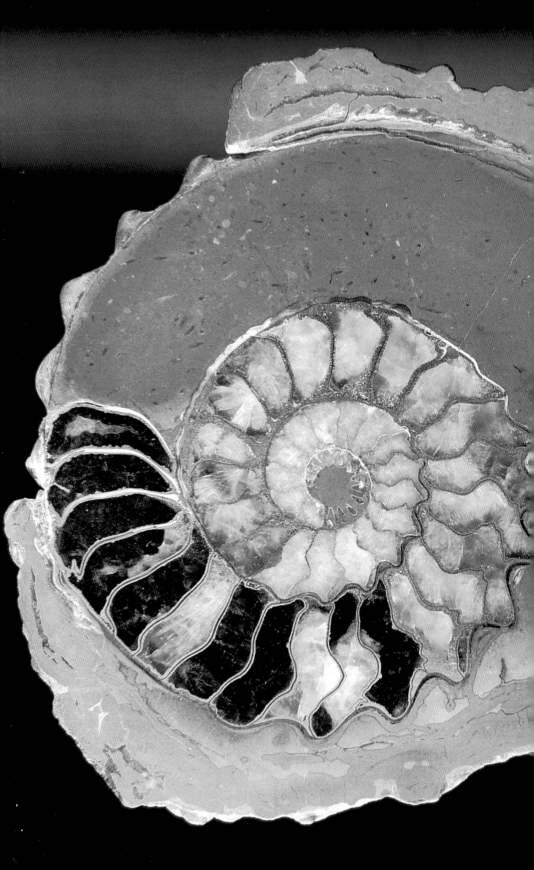

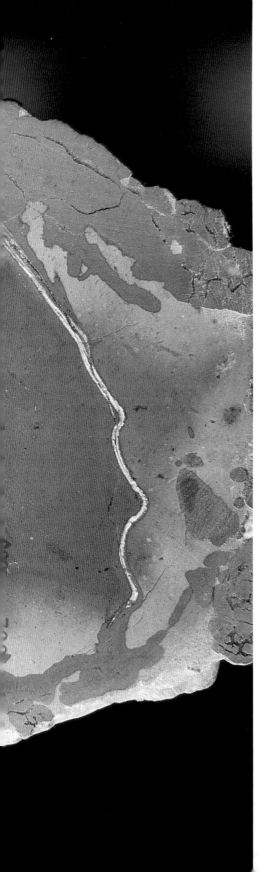

FOSSIL
COLLECTOR'S
HANDBOOK

Finding · Identifying · Preparing · Displaying

Gerhard Lichter

Sterling Publishing Co., Inc. New York

Picture credits: 220 4-color photographs by the author and 39 2-color illustrations by Helga and Hans Bröker, after samples by the author (37) and Andreas Dauenhauer (2).
Photo on page 1: The beautiful Altmühltal with its Jurassic sponge remnants, near Dollnstein, an ideal place for fossil enthusiasts.
Photo on title pages: Cross-section of a fossilized ammonite, *Pleuroceras*, 3½ inches (9 cm) long. It had been embedded in mud for 180 million years. The shell remnants are pyritized, and the chambered inside is filled with calcite crystals.

Translated by Elisabeth E. Reinersmann

Library of Congress Cataloging-in-Publication Data

Lichter, Gerhard.
    [Fossilien bergen, präparieren, ausstellen. English]
    Fossil collector's handbook: finding, identifying, preparing,
displaying / Gerhard Lichter ; [translated by Elisabeth E.
Reinersmann]
    p.   cm.
    Includes bibliographical references and index.
    ISBN 0-8069-0350-3
    1. Fossils—Collection and preservation—Handbooks, manuals, etc.
I. Title.
QE718.L5313   1993
560'.75—dc20   93-24783
                                        CIP

10 9 8 7 6 5 4 3 2

Published 1993 by Sterling Publishing Company, Inc.
387 Park Avenue South, New York, N.Y. 10016
Originally published and © 1986 in Germany by
Franckh-Kosmos Verlags-GmbH under the title *Fossilien
bergen, präparieren, ausstellen: Geräte und Techniken*
English translation and new material
© 1993 by Sterling Publishing Company, Inc.
Distributed in Canada by Sterling Publishing
% Canadian Manda Group, P.O. Box 920, Station U
Toronto, Ontario, Canada M8Z 5P9
Distributed in Great Britain and Europe by Cassell PLC
Villiers House, 41/47 Strand, London WC2N 5JE, England
Distributed in Australia by Capricorn Link Ltd.
P.O. Box 665, Lane Cove, NSW 2066
Printed and bound in Hong Kong
All rights reserved

Sterling ISBN 0-8069-0350-3

Contents

List of 2-Color Illustrations and Tables

Illustrations

Tables

Preface

This book is meant to ease the way from being merely a "friend of fossils" to becoming a "collector of fossils." It is the record of a fossil collector who was fortunate enough to have support not only from his family but also from his many like-minded friends. In addition, I had access to technical guides and to both old and modern scientific literature. The photographs of the fossils in this book are from my own collection. With the exception of a few samples, I personally collected all of the fossils.

Each fossil is only as good as the preparation that goes into it. This is why I have listed so many simple, proven, and effective tips and methods.

I hope this book will bring to you, who are reading this book in English, enjoyment and relaxation. The practical tips presented here will add to your success as you collect and preserve fossils. Since fossilized deposits result in similar types of rock formation all over the world—such as shale, sandstone, chalk, or limestone—the tips in this book are useful for fossil collectors everywhere. References to particular types of fossils found in Germany are merely examples.

Because the book is organized according to distinct types of fossil-bearing rocks (distinctions even lay people are able to make, such as hard, soft, or layered rock formations), the examples can also be used for those rocks that are not specifically discussed. I have included in this guide all the information necessary for a fossil collector. For instance, I discuss the many different types of fossilization, the fossils found in different rock formations, and I give a list of the essential tools and how to use them.

This information is accompanied by many color photos and drawings. We have included color plates of fossils in the United States and numerous references to rock formations and also well-known collecting localities in the United States. I trust these will be helpful as you begin your journey to becoming a successful fossil collector. In this endeavor I wish you good luck. Much detailed information about the life of animals and plants in ancient times is still hidden; many puzzles are not yet solved. The drawings, therefore, can only give approximations of the forms and shapes of early life.

References to tables, illustrations, and photographs found within the text serve to make a harmonious connection between written and visual information, increasing the didactic value of the book. Numbers in parentheses in the text give the color plate and color photo number. For instance (15–5) refers the reader to color plate 15, and to photo 5 within that plate.

My thanks to Dr. Karl Beurlen for his expert advice, for reading the manuscript and for writing the foreword to the German edition of the book. I am also grateful to the publishers for their help, support, and layout of the book. For their advice and kind help in the preparation of this book, my thanks go to the following: Carin Kirsten, Ulm; Roland Kirsten, Ulm; Reinhard Kuhn, Günzburg; Gerd H. Leichter, Bad Salzdetfurth; Dr. Thaddäus Liske, Biberach/Riss; Dr. Heinz Malz, Forschungsinstitut und Naturmuseum, Senkenberg, Frankfurt am Main; Dr. Max Urlichs, Staatliches Museum für Naturkunde, Stuttgart; and Professor Dr. Peter S. Wu, Osaka, Japan.

—Gerhard Lichter

Geologic Timetable for Animals and Plants

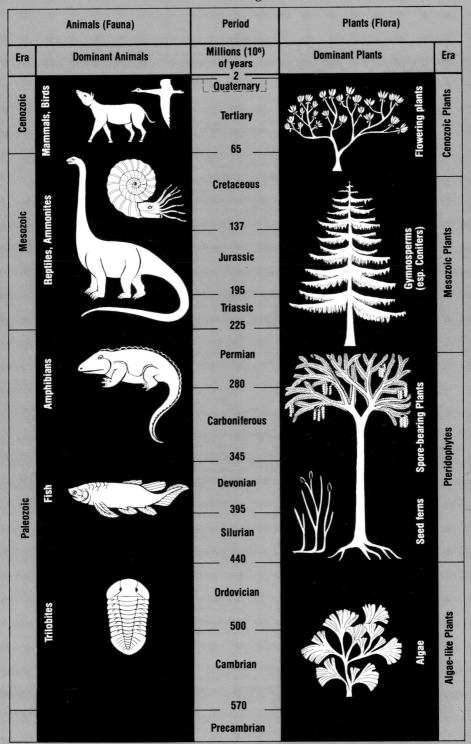

Animals (Fauna)		Period	Plants (Flora)	
Era	Dominant Animals	Millions (10^6) of years	Dominant Plants	Era
Cenozoic	Mammals, Birds	2 Quaternary Tertiary 65	Flowering plants	Cenozoic Plants
Mesozoic	Reptiles, Ammonites	Cretaceous 137 Jurassic 195 Triassic 225	Gymnosperms (esp. Conifers)	Mesozoic Plants
Paleozoic	Amphibians	Permian 280 Carboniferous 345	Spore-bearing Plants	Pteridophytes
	Fish	Devonian 395 Silurian 440	Seed ferns	
	Trilobites	Ordovician 500 Cambrian 570 Precambrian	Algae	Algae-like Plants

Introduction

Fossil Collectors and Their Territory

No one is born a fossil collector. Somewhere, sometime, sooner or later, the person was introduced to the remains of prehistoric events. In the beginning, just for the fun of it, the collector might pick up an unusual fossil in the form of a rock, become curious, and want to identify the find. By the time he or she learns that this object came from a distant past, the future collector is hooked. He or she will want to understand why a particular region has been formed the way it has and will learn to recognize which rocks are hidden under a particular cover of vegetation. All of a sudden, different layers of the earth become visible, perhaps on a steep bank of a stream, at an excavation site for a foundation, or during road construction.

Igneous rocks, which have been formed either from magma or in the lower layers of the earth under high pressure and high temperatures, are not the place to look for fossils. Only in sedimentary rocks can the collector find remnants of the world of plants (flora) and animals (fauna), and even there, only if the organisms have been quickly embedded under favorable circumstances—for instance, in deposits on the floor of prehistoric oceans. Fossils from earlier land regions usually are limited to specific sites; for instance, former lake beds, where many animal remnants have been carried by water. Typical examples are the brown-coal region of Geiseltal (Geisel Valley) near Halle and the oil-shale region in Messel near Darmstadt.

The fossil collector needs patience and endurance, and experience, lots of experience, in order to recognize a fossil-bearing rock from very slim evidence. Seldom will one come across a fossil displayed in flawless beauty, just waiting to be collected.

Fossil-bearing rocks are relatively easy to find at large construction sites, where road construction is in progress, or at sites where reservoirs are being built, on riverbanks and steep slopes after a frost, and on sites of either old or new landslides, which often yield a rich harvest of many different fossils.

When on a fossil hunt, a collector concentrates on finding rocks that most likely will bear fossils, breaks the rocks apart with a hammer into manageable pieces, and tries not to damage the fossils within. Since rocks have distinct ways of breaking apart, the collector soon learns how to carefully pack all the relevant pieces for the trip home. The

Plate 1
1. Manganese oxide, malachite, and azurite dendrites from Altenmittlau, Hesse, 2¾ inches (7 cm).
2. Black manganese oxide dendrites on an ammonite, *Glochiceras*, 1⅛ inches (2.5 cm), from the Jurassic Kimmeridgian stage (Malm gamma) in Geisingen/Danube.
3. Stylolite, woodlike structures in limestone, here in shell limestone from Haigerloch, Württemberg.
4. Reddish-brown, 2-inch (5 cm) dendrites, mosslike iron oxide deposits, on a limestone plate from Solnhofen.
5. Ripplelike 5½-inch (14 cm) markings on the surface of limestone of Jurassic Hettangian stage (Liassic alpha 2) near Schwäbisch Gmünd.
6. Sea grass slate from the Jurassic Toarcian stage (Liassic epsilon) from the Swabian Alps, 4⅜ inches (11 cm). What looks like stems are worm borings.
[See Table 5, Jurassic Classification, for Jurassic stages—ed.]

location and rock formation where the sample was found are carefully recorded on a piece of paper with an indelible pen. After the collector returns home, usually very tired, he or she can put the "treasures" aside without worry, saving further work on them on a rainy, wintry day.

Pseudofossils and Trace Fossils

While hunting for fossils, one comes across many objects that seem to look like fossils. A beginner may easily become confused by these. This happened to me on my first fossil outing. While on a trip alone, I took a break and for two hours began to randomly search through layers of clay. I found small pieces of pyrite and, embedded in clay, large hard rocks resembling the shape of a fish. Proudly and carefully I packed everything for the trip home. A geologist from Stuttgart who I asked for an evaluation of my "fossil" treasure wrote that they were concretions, so-called phosphoritic nodules. Since then, I have had to give much the same information to many a beginner, always trying to do so with the same professional earnestness that Dr. Beurlen accorded me when I started out. After careful examination of a sample, he said to me, "This is a small piece of rock." All the same, my phosphoritic nodules have a permanent place in my collection. Of course, there are other pseudofossils. For instance,

the woodlike limestone formation (1–3) is most likely a diagenetic sediment deposit that developed during rock formation or water-worn rock. The much admired "small trees," "flowers," or mosslike structures in the limestone block from Solnhofen (1–4) are in particularly good condition. Such structures also can be found on small ammonites (1–2), on crystallized rocks, or as part of minerals, for example, imprints on barite and river spar (1–1); or on limestone shells. These fantastically beautiful dentrites are usually formed by crystallized solutions of iron oxide (reddish-brown) or manganese oxide (black) that seeped through narrow cracks into the rocks.

Fossilized sand dunes and ripplelike markings (1–5) appear as pictures of drifting or fine-grained beach sand. It has been suggested that these ripplelike markings are evidence of a quiet body of water that was exposed to a gentle wind many millions of years ago. Structures from the Black Jurassic period, found in layers of clay that resemble fine or distinct branchings, are borings created by mud-eating or mud-boring organisms (1–6). Large indentations (2–1), dating from the Jurassic period, are most certainly traces of a dinosaur's footprints.

Traces of organisms are also preserved in very find sand—most likely, traces of wormlike organisms or very impressive evidence of small starfish. The borings of crawling animals and the cavities of starfish filled in with sediment and subsequently hardened into solid forms.

Plate 2
1. Footprints of a three-toed *Megalosauropus teutonias*, a giant dinosaur, are 24 inches (60 cm) in diameter, with footprints resembling those of an elephant. From the Jurassic Malm epoch, Kimmeridgian stage from Barkhausen in the Wiehen mountains.
2. Traces of resting starfish *Asteriatites lumbricalis* Schlotheim, 1⅛ inches (3 cm), from sandstone of the Jurassic Hettangian stage (Liassic alpha 2), near Frankenhofen, Württemberg.
3–5. *Dactylioceras* ammonites from the Jurassic Toarcian stage (Liassic epsilon) in various forms. **3:** Calcified, with an intact body, from the region of Forchheim, 3⅛ inches (8 cm). **4:** Compressed calcified ammonite in Poseidon Slate near Holzmaden, 4⅜ inches (11 cm). **5:** Flattened, with chalklike shell near Hesselberg, Franconian Jura, 3⅛ inches (8 cm).

When Remnants of Living Organisms Become Fossils

Sediments accumulating over millions of years undergo something similar to an aging process: clay becomes shale; lime mud changes to limestone; and sand ages into sandstone. Remnants of organisms embedded in sediment participate in this process of geological change, called *diagenesis*. The process of fossilization continues to this day. The result of this process depends to a large extent on the composition of the organism, the circumstances at the time it was embedded, and the specific fossilization process. In other words, depending on the situation, similar organisms can fossilize differently.

Ammonites from the Jurassic lower Toar-

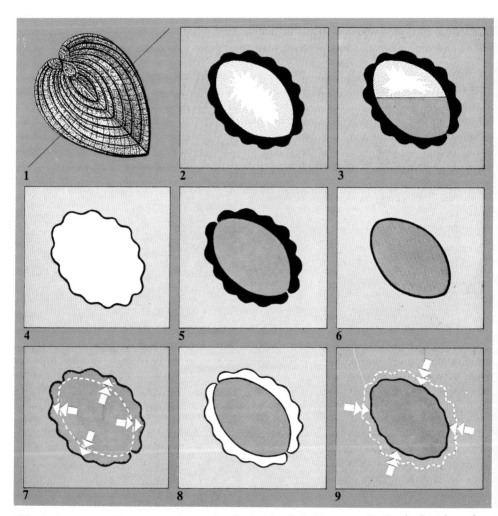

Illus. 1. An example of the process of fossilization of a shell. **1.** Shell with cross-section line. **2.** Crystal growth. **3.** Water level (line). **4.** Fossil cavity and imprint. **5.** Preservation of shell with *steinkern*. **6.** *Steinkern*. **7.** Impression. **8.** Shell cavity with *steinkern* and external mold. **9.** Natural cast of external mold.

14

Table 1. Geologic Time Units

Era	Period (m.y.)	European Epoch (Series)	European Age (Stage)	North American Epoch (Series)
CENOZOIC	Quaternary — 2		(see Table 2)	
CENOZOIC	Tertiary — 65	Early	(see Table 2)	
CENOZOIC	Tertiary — 65	Late		
MESOZOIC	Cretaceous — 137	Upper	(see Table 4)	
MESOZOIC	Cretaceous — 137	Lower		
MESOZOIC	Jurassic — 195	Malm (Upper)	(see Table 5)	Morrison
MESOZOIC	Jurassic — 195	Dogger (Middle)		
MESOZOIC	Jurassic — 195	Liassic (Lower)		
MESOZOIC	Triassic — 225	Keuper (Upper)		Pardonet
MESOZOIC	Triassic — 225	Muschelkalk [Shell limestone] (Middle)		Grey Beds / Liardian
MESOZOIC	Triassic — 225	Buntsandstein [Colored sandstone] (Lower)		Toad
PALEOZOIC	Permian — 280	Zechstein (Upper)		Ochoan / Guadalupe (Texas)
PALEOZOIC	Permian — 280	Red-layered (Lower)		Leonardian / Wolfcampian (Texas)
PALEOZOIC	Carboniferous — 345	Upper	Stephanian / Westphalian / Namurian	Pennsylvanian
PALEOZOIC	Carboniferous — 345	Lower	Viséan / Tournaisian	Mississippian
PALEOZOIC	Devonian — 395	Upper	Wocklum / Dasberg / Hemberg / Nehden } Famennian; Adorf (Frasnian)	Bradfordian / Chautauquan / Senecan
PALEOZOIC	Devonian — 395	Middle	Givetian / Eifelian	Erian
PALEOZOIC	Devonian — 395	Lower	Ems / Siegen / Gedinnian	Ulsterian
PALEOZOIC	Silurian — 440	Ludlovian (Upper)		Cayugan
PALEOZOIC	Silurian — 440	Wenlockian (Middle)		Niagaran
PALEOZOIC	Silurian — 440	Llandoverian (Lower)		Albionian
PALEOZOIC	Ordovician — 500		Ashgillian / Caradocian	Cincinnatian / Trentonian
PALEOZOIC	Ordovician — 500		Llandellian / Llanvirnian	Mohawkian
PALEOZOIC	Ordovician — 500		Arenigian / Tremadocian	Canadian
PALEOZOIC	Cambrian — 570	Upper		Croixian
PALEOZOIC	Cambrian — 570	Middle		Albertan
PALEOZOIC	Cambrian — 570	Lower		Waucoban
PALEOZOIC	Precambrian			

m.y. = millions (10^6) of years.

cian stage Liassic epsilon (see Table 5) are typical examples: calcified ammonites with body form intact (2–3); compressed, paper-thin remnants found in Poseidon Slate (2–4); and chalky images on dark layers of clay (2–5).

The soft tissues of an organism are easily destroyed, either by being exposed to air (whenever sufficient oxygen is present) or by decomposition (when little oxygen is there but carbon dioxide and bitumen are present, as in the formation of oil). Hard substances, on the other hand, deteriorate much more slowly. They break, are ground up, or are dissolved by water.

Acidic lime springs (such as those in the Bära Valley or near Gutmadingen in the Western Swabian Alps) often carry highly concentrated solutions of lime. The lime, deposited as lime sinter, often can cover organisms like leaves within hours. Molds created by this process are evidence of fossilization (3–1).

Soft tissues or organisms without hard shells, such as worms, are seldom found in the form of fossils. At most, we see their borings or their tracks as evidence of their existence (1–6). The exceptions in the United States are fossils like the bot fly larvae from the Tertiary Eocene in the Green River Formation in Uintah County, Utah and the soft-body impressions of worms from the Carboniferous period in Mazon Creek, Illinois

(7). Organisms with hard body parts usually leave behind only those parts in the form of fossils. Extraordinary circumstances make it possible for organisms to survive intact; for instance, the remnants of a saber-tooth tiger, smilodon, have been found in the asphalt pits in Rancho La Brea, near Los Angeles, California.

A fossil collector only learns about the many different types of fossilization through practical experience (see Illus. 1). Fossils found in sandlike deposits that date from a more recent past often are unchanged from the time they were alive, like the shell of a snail embedded in Miocene marl, which filled with mud (3–2), or the snail shell in Plate 4.

Aragonite shells often dissolve or change into more stable calcite shells, which do not dissolve as easily (3–3). Whenever we deal with an original shell or with one that has crystallized into another substance, we speak of "shell preservation." In claylike layers, this change often results in the formation of a chalklike mold (3–4). If the cavity of a shell is filled in with mud in the course of being imbedded, what remains after the original shell has been destroyed and the mud hardens is called a *steinkern* (3–5). However, it is not always possible for mud, clay, or sand to fill all of the cavity of a shell. We often find that during the fossilization process, crystallization has taken place in the hollow portion of

Plate 3

1. Impressions of beech leaves, 2⅜ inches (6 cm), formed in recent lime sinter near Bärental, in the Swabian Alps.
2. *Coretus cornu* (Brogniart), 1⅜ inches (3 cm), with a calcified shell, from the upper freshwater deposits near Zwiefalten, Swabian Alps.

3. *Plagiostoma gigantea* from the Jurassic Sinemurian (Liassic alpha 3), a calcified, ¼-inch-thick (6 mm) shell, showing a *steinkern* in the broken-off portion.
4. *Pleuroceras spinatum* (Brugiere), 2 inches (5 cm) wide, from the Jurassic Pliensbachian (Liassic delta), from the Unterstürming in the Franconian Mountains. The body is intact, and the original shell has changed to a chalklike substance.
5. *Steinkern* of *Diceras*, 2¾ inches (7 cm), a thick-shelled bivalve from the Jurassic Tithonian stage (Malm zeta) from Grossmehring.

16

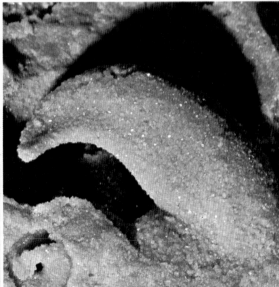

the cavity. Mussels, belemnites, ammonites, and other fossils that either broke accidentally or have been sawn in half often show the presence of very beautiful crystals (5–1, 5–2). The partially filled cavity of a shell gives accurate information on the position of the organism on the ground at the time it was embedded. Before it hardens, the surface of the sediment or mud inside the cavity settles and creates a horizontal plane. When fossilization is complete, the horizontal plane

Manticoceras intumescens (Upper Devonian), Prümer Slope, 2¼″ (5.5 cm). The mold of a shell and a copy (*right*) made from it.

is called the "water level." This happens with ammonites, brachiopods, and sea urchins (5–3).

Whenever a shell dissolves during the process of fossilization, while the sediments in the inside form the so-called *steinkern*, the exterior of original shell leaves a distinct impression, a natural mold, on the ground where the shell came to rest. These impressions or molds don't form a *steinkern*. However, a duplicate of a fossil can be recreated by pouring plastic material into the natural mold (see the photo of a mold and shell at the left).

If a shell dissolves slowly, it is possible for the contours of the shell to leave an accurate impression on the outside of the *steinkern* called a cast. Such casts of bivalves, ammonites, and other thin-shelled organisms usually are easy to find (6–2). It is also possible to find casts that show distinct impressions from the inside of a shell. These casts are called *steinkern casts (Prägesteinkern)*. In the case of a very thin-shelled organism, the cast and the *steinkern* cast are often identical like those from ammonites.

Many chemical and physical processes influence an organism before it changes into a fossil. Hard parts, for instance, retain their shape but not their original substance. If the hard parts have an organic base, like the chitinous or hard parts of trilobites or insects they are mineralized.

It is important for the fossil collector to understand, for instance, the process of calcification through calcite. In the process of dolomitization (which can be observed in reef limestone), fossil structures are totally dissolved, changing from chalk ($CaCO_3$ into $CaMg(CO_3)_2$. Silicification of fossil that contain silicic acid is another example of excellent preservation. It is assumed that silicic acid was washed out of porous gravel

Plate 4

Snail shell of the *Vasum horridum*, 3½ inches (9 cm), dating from the Tertiary Pliocene, near LaBelle, Florida; it shows how a marvelous fossil, extracted from soft deposits, can be collected and prepared.

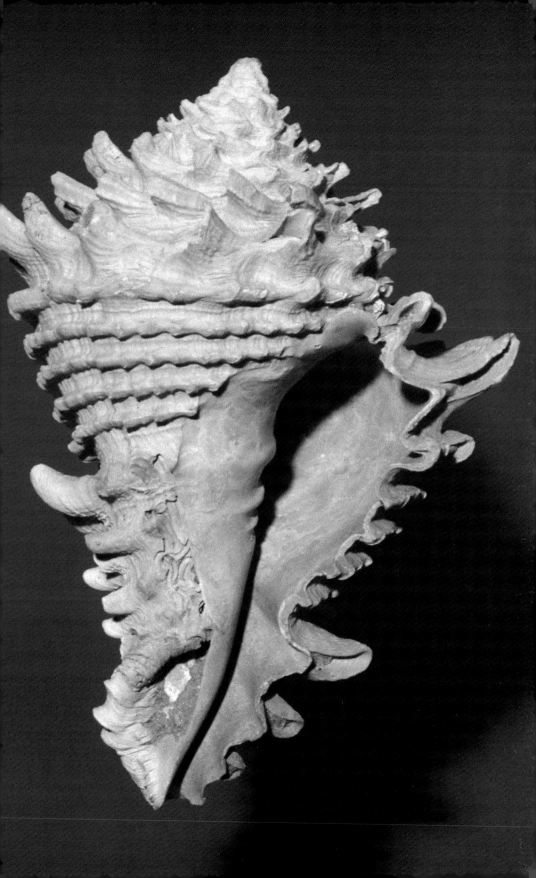

layers during the Upper Jurassic period and replaced with limestone (calcium carbonate). Sponge stumps from the Jurassic period are typical examples of the results of such a process. Bivalves, brachiopods, and other fossils absorbed such liquified silicic acid (8–2). Silicification of the flint sea-urchin from the Cretaceous period is probably another example (6–4). Amorphous flint was produced during the same period, also by silicic acid. The silicified tree stumps in Yellowstone National Park are another example.

Fossil collectors are excited when they find shiny, golden-colored, pyritic fossils. During pyritization, hydrogen sulfide, present in claylike sediments, reacts with iron—often while the sediments are still fresh—yielding hard pyrite (FeS_2). In a less stable form, it is called marcasite. The rather rapid replacement of organic substances via pyritization

produces very beautiful fossils (15–5), where the shape of the body of the organism is well preserved. Clay and clay-marl deposits in the beginning contain relatively high amounts of water, which slowly evaporates in the course of fossilization. These deposits are compressed, often until they are only one-tenth or even one-twentieth of their original thickness. This process is called *pelomorphosis*. Fossils embedded in deposits that are subject to pelomorphosis also alter their shape: they break, stretch, or are compressed, becoming paper-thin. A typical example is the Poseidon Slate found in Holzmaden from the Toarcian period of the Black Jurassic, or Liassic epsilon (29–1, 29–2, 29–3).

Often remains of organisms are damaged either during the time they are embedded in sediment or later; and sometimes damage occurs even after fossilization is complete.

Plate 5 (page 20)
1. Crystal growth, 3½ inches (9 cm), in the cavity of a mollusk shell, *Ctenostreon pectiniformis* (Schlotheim), from the Jurassic, Bajocian (Dogger delta), near Wartenberg, Danube.
2. A cavity of 2⅜ inches (6 cm) inside an ammonite is filled with different crystals from the Jurassic Upper Dogger in the Wiehen Mountains.
3. Water level inside sea-urchin *Echinolampas kleini* (Goldfuss), 2 inches (5 cm), from the Upper Oligocene period, Doberg/Bünde.

Plate 6 (page 22)
1. Cavity of the coral *Stylina*, 2 inches long (5 cm), from the Jurassic Tithonian (Malm zeta) near Laisacker, Franconian Jura.
2. *Steinkern* cast, 2 inches long (5 cm), from a member of the pecten family, from the Jurassic Kimmeridgian (Malm delta) near Biburg, Franconian Jura.
3. Natural cast of an arca, 2 inches long (5 cm), from the upper sea deposits near Ursendorf, Upper Swabia.
4. Flint sea-urchin, 2¾ inches long (7 cm), from the Upper Cretaceous period, in amorphous flint from the island Möen.
5. Deformed belemnite, 4¾ inches long (12 cm), from the Middle Liassic, found in the western part of the Swabian Alps.

Plate 7 (page 23)
Siderite concretions, dating from the Carboniferous-Pennsylvanian period, from Francis Creek Shale, Essex, Illinois, were treated with the hot-cold therapy. They are then easier to open up and may contain surprising fossils of organisms that otherwise would have barely been able to survive, such as worms. The fossils shown in Plate 7 were found and prepared by Prof. Dr. Wu.
1. Leaf whorls from a horsetail plant, *Annularia sphenopsis*, ¾ inch (2 cm) each.
2. *Fossundecimus konecniorum*, 2 inches (5 cm), an early worm.
3. *Coprinoscolex alligimus*, 1 inch (2.5 cm), a primitive leech.
4. Phylum unknown, *Tullimonstrum gregarium*, 4 inches (10 cm).

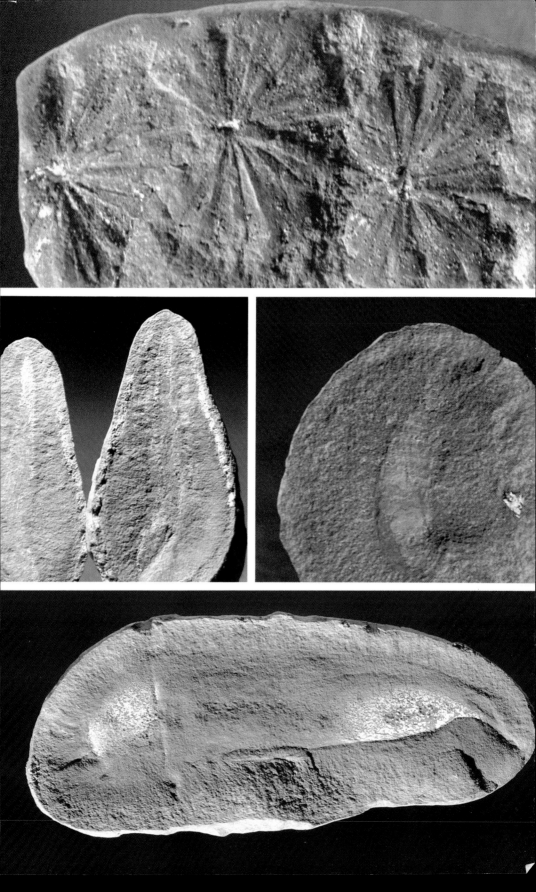

The belemnite shown in Plate 6 (6–5) shows such deformation. Many compressed ammonites are further examples of this process. However, by far the greatest damage to fossils occurs when rocks are formed. The ammonite shown in Plate 9 (9–1), found in the Alps at 6,500 feet (2,000 m) elevation, from the Lower or Black Jurassic period (Liassic), has sustained relatively little damage from tectonic pressures. Fossils deformed by such forces are difficult to identify.

Hard rock nodules located in relatively soft sediments are easy to find. The collector should not overlook them, because such concretions often develop around fossil remains. Depending on the character of the sediment, typical concretions are made of limestone, clay, iron pyrites, or phosphate of lime (see Plates 7 and Plates 33 through 36).

It is said that fossils seldom retain the color of the original plant or animal organism. However, they make up for this loss with many different shapes and forms, and with the color of the material that is produced— whether pyritized, brass-colored, or copper-

gold. Some shells change into white chalk o crystallized chalk in many different varia tions, some lighter and some darker. Some times fossils take on the same color as the surrounding sediment. Then again, arranged in different layers, they show a contrasting display of colors: yellow, white, red, brown or black plant remnants deposited on gray yellow, red, or white rocks; or white, black or brown fossilized fish.

Scales from 50-million-year-old crocodile fishes are fine examples of harmonious col ors, shapes, and delicate markings (8–1) Some ammonites shimmer like opal, because the outer layer of their shell was lost but a portion of the mother-of-pearl layer re mained. The ammonite *Leioceras opalinum* (8–3) was named for this opalescence. Cal cified ammonites from the region near Soln hofen often shimmer in every color of the rainbow when exposed to sunlight. Ammo nites from the Upper Cretaceous with a shel like mother of pearl, found in the United States in Pierre Shale, are among the most impressive of opalized fossils (see Plate 46)

Plate 8
1. Ganoid scales, 2 to 2¾ inches long (5 to 7 mm), from *Lepisosteus strausi*, a crocodile fish from the Eocene, from Messel.
2. *Ismenia pectunculoidea* (Schlotheim), ¾ inch wide (2 cm), on a cockscomb oyster *Arctostrea gregarea* (Sowerby), silicified, from the Nattheimer layers of the Jurassic Malm epsilon, (Kim meridgian stage).
3. Opalized shell of the ammonite *Leioceras opalinum* (Reinecke), 3⅛ inches wide (8 cm), from the Jurassic Aalenian stage (Dogger alpha), near Heiningen/Göppingen.

Collecting and Preparing Fossils

The first attempts at fossil collection are best undertaken with the help of an experienced fossil collector. Introductory courses and group excursions will give the beginner the basic knowledge necessary for success. The beginner will be able to get information on fossil-containing locations from museums of natural science, from professionals, from professional journals, from local fossil collectors, and from field guides to specific regions and maps (scale of 1:25,000). It is important to always obey local regulations and to obtain permission when entering privately owned land. For some areas, geological maps are available showing the type of earth layers that lie under specific vegetation.

Fossils Embedded in Soft Layers

Fossils Embedded in Sand

Lucky and well-advised is the person who has been able to win his or her family's support for the hobby of finding and collecting of fossils. The best locations to look in sand are ones where Tertiary sand is still relatively loose, for instance, sand pits in the upper marine deposits in the Upper Swabian region. This location is safe and has an abundance of small fossils. Children in particular are easy to inspire. Every shark tooth they find will cause great excitement (9–2). Shark teeth glisten when wet, and it is easy to find them by the handful after a rain (11–1). In the United States, the beginner will find beautiful specimens in the fossil-rich sandstone deposits from the Tertiary Pliocene period in La Belle, Florida. These fossils are comparatively easy to prepare (see Plate 4).

Shark teeth need no preservation; they can be displayed the way they are. Other fossils, however, need work before they are stable, like the small, spongelike, round, antler-shaped or raspberry-shaped remains of a bryozoan colony (11–2) and bivalves, which are usually preserved in the form of a *steinkern* or a *steinkern* cast, which might be covered with sand and wedged in a piece of slag.

Fossils embedded in sandstone usually leave clues as to their presence. Use a hammer or a chisel to reduce the sandstone to a manageable size and, after deciding which ones it is worthwhile keeping, carefully wrap your treasures and make a note of the location. The more delicate work can be done at home.

A region near Ulm clearly shows the dividing line between saltwater and freshwater. It was here that I found an abundance of small snails, as well as larger snails, which were deposited in fine-grained layers of sandstone—sometimes several yards thick—during the late Tertiary period (12–1). I packed a sufficiently large piece of the wet

Table 2. Tertiary Classification

Period	Epoch	European Stage (Age)	Deposits in Upper Swabia	California	Gulf Region
Quaternary	Holocene			Hallian	Citronelle
	Pleistocene			Wheelerian	
— 2 m.y.					
Tertiary	Pliocene		Upper freshwater deposits (younger)	Venturian Repettian Delmontian	Pascagoula Yorktown-Duplin
	Miocene	Sarmatian	Upper freshwater deposits (older) Kirchberger Layers	Mohnian	
		Tortonian			
		Serravalian	Grimmelfinger granular sand	Luisian	St. Mary's Choptank
		Langhian	Upper marine deposits		
		Burdigalian		Relizian	Calvert
		Aquitanian	Lower freshwater deposits	Saucesian	Anahuac
	Oligocene	Upper	Lower marine deposits	Zemorrian	Chickasawhay-Frio
		Middle			
		Lower			Vicksburg
	Eocene			Refugian Narizian Ulatisian Penutian Bulitian	Jackson-Ocala Claiborne Wilcox/Sabine
	Paleocene			Ynezian Danian	Aquia Midway
— 65 m.y. Cretaceous					

m.y. = millions (10^6) of years.

sandstone in newspaper.

I unpacked carefully at home and let it dry uncovered. With the help of a knife, needle, and brush, the careful search for embedded snails could begin (12–1). Since snail shells lift off easily, it is important to proceed with great caution. In the end, I had unearthed a small but typical fossil for the location (12–3), which could be preserved with the help of fixative or spray varnish.

Near Los Angeles, California, collectors have found very well preserved, 65-million-year-old starfish in luminous sandstone deposits from the Tertiary Paleocene period (see Plate 51). Among other fossils, beautiful sea-urchins are found in dense sandstone deposits from the Tertiary Miocene period near San Diego and in the Cuyana Valley, California. These are relatively easy to prepare (see Plates 20, 21, and 51). Similar deposits, containing sea urchins from the Tertiary Eocene period, are also found near Tivola, Houston County, Georgia. Hard sandstone deposits from the Cretaceous are also found in South Dakota (Dakota Sandstone). In England, similar sandstone deposits exist in the Bagshot Sands near London and in the Headen Hill Sands near Hampshire.

Fossils Embedded in Soft Marl

Locations that have more or less soft layers of marl (those containing chalk and clay particles) are found in stone formations dating from the Tertiary period; however, I have also found them in the Jura of southern Germany. In the United States, fossils are also found in marl deposits, for instance, from the Carboniferous Mississippian period near Crawfordsville, Indiana (see Plate 53), in the Paint Creek Shale near Millstat, Illinois (see Plate 60), and from the Silurian period near Waldron, Indiana (see Plate 60). From the somewhat harder marl chalk, from the Devonian period, near Utah, come completely preserved trilobites (see Plate 10). Similar deposits from the Devonian period are found in Ohio. (See Plate 10).

There is no recipe for how to split these layers. Generally, only the individual layers themselves can be separated, one layer at a time, and then lifted off; sometimes separation occurs where fossils or leaves are embedded. Much luck is involved in unearthing well-preserved leaves that are somewhat typical of their species. Public construction sites may expose layers of plant remnants from the Tertiary period. If that is the case, it will be easy to separate those fossil-carrying layers. The marl is cut (a safe distance away from the fossil), and the layers are lifted off, using either a hammer (13–2) or a wide chisel. Care should be taken that the layer of marl is thick enough. Marl dries into a very hard substance; therefore, do as much of the above-described cutting as possible on location. Crumbs remaining on the fossil should be carefully removed before the marl dries; a small brush is very effective for this purpose (13–1). Similar plant remnants are found in England from the Jurassic, Lower and Middle Estaurine series/Bajocian, and the Upper Estaurine series/Bathonian near Yorkshire.

Identifying fossils and plant remains is very difficult. If possible, take the negative impression of plants (13–3, 13–4). They might show some structures that are important for later identification. Thin marl plates with impressions of leaves should be allowed to dry out slowly. Particular caution should be taken when handling Cretaceous shells. They only become stable after they have dried out and have been chemically protected with a fixative.

Snails in marl from a Tertiary layer were embedded without any stratification. The extra-fine grain of the mud that covered the objects was a good protective cover. However, this material attracts a lot of moisture. It is considerably lighter when dry. A dental explorer can be carefully used to locate the snails; or water can be used to soften the dried out material, which can then be scraped off. My reward for all this painstaking work was the uncovering of tiny, 15-million-year-old snails with spotted and finely sculptured shells (14–1, 14–2).

In France, I came across almost chalklike,

Plate 9
1. Ammonite, 6⅜ inches (16 cm), deformed by tectonic pressure, from the Jurassic, Lower Liassic (Sinemurian stage), from a stone plate near Weidring, Tyrol.
2. In search of shark teeth in the upper marine deposits near Saulgau, Upper Swabia.

white deposits from the Miocene period. They contained remnants of leaves and fish, which presented a striking picture on the white background (14–4). The material was wet and heavy, but it became as light as a feather after it dried out.

Fossils embedded in the somewhat heavier marl from the Black Jurassic gamma (Lower Pliensbachian stage) are very easy to prepare in a relatively short time. It is best to allow the marl to dry out slowly. Afterwards, dried material can easily be removed with a brush.

Table 3. Chalk–Clay Blends*

Percent of Chalk	Name	Percent of Clay
95%	Limestone (high percentage)	5%
85%	Marllike chalk	15%
75%	Marl chalk	25%
65%	Chalk marl	35%
35%	Marl	65%
25%	Clay marl	75%
15%	Marl clay	85%
5%	Marllike clay	95%
0%	Clay (high percentage)	100%

*according to Correns.

Spraying the fossil for preservation purposes is seldom necessary; however, interesting optical contrasts can be created against the light marl (14–3) if you choose to do so.

Fossils Embedded in Layers of Clay

Layers of clay harden over time due to the pressure exerted by deposits above. An increase in chalk in these layers produces clay marl (see the table at left), which is composed of very small particles. When fresh, these layers are gray to blue-black in color. Over time, the continuous pressure produces the much harder, slaty shale. Typical layers of clay from England are: London Clay (Upper Paleocene–Lower Eocene), Oxford Clay, and Kimmeridge Clay (Upper Jurassic).

Fossil-rich slaty shale contains about everything a fossil collector's heart could desire. Since this material has developed as a result of sediments being deposited in rather even layers, these layers are easy to separate with a hammer or a chisel along the bedding plane. Start with a large piece and—without rushing—break it into smaller pieces. If the rock sample originates from the Black Jurassic delta, or Upper Pliensbachian stage, you might want to look first for one of the attractive, pyritic fossil *Amaltheus*, an ammonite named after Jupiter's goat (15–1).

Very often pyritized fossils are present between the rock layers. However, most of the time only a portion of the fossil is visible. It can be identified by its shape, or you may notice the pyrite crystal that has formed around the fossil. A "pyrite fossil" that obviously has been well preserved can be care-

Plate 10

1, 2. The trilobite *Flexicalymene*, 1 inch (2.5 cm) long, from the Devonian period in Utah, was carefully extracted from marl chalk and prepared.
3. This tiny, blind trilobite, *Peronopsis interstrictus*, ⅜ inch (1 cm) long, attached to limestone, was found in the Wheeler Formation, from the Cambrian period, House Range, Millard County, Utah. It was preserved in perfect condition.
4. Trilobite *Phacops rana* Miller, 1 inch (2.5 cm) long, from Devonian silica shale, from Sylvania, Ohio. Thanks to careful preparation with a needle, this specimen is in good condition.

fully lifted out with an asparagus knife. The tool is brushed into the sand. I also use this tool to reach specimens that are more deeply embedded (32–1). When first encountering fossils they seem of uniform gray color. Fragile pyrite ammonites from the Lower Cretaceous period near Hannover, which break very easily, usually have a whitish, opalized shell (15–2). Pyrites (FeS_2), the most common form of pyrite, often creates a protective shield around a fossil. It can replace the original shell, making the fossil more stable. Because of its hardness (6 to 6.5), pyrite is less fragile. Nevertheless, pyrite fossils (particularly the bigger, thin-shelled ones) should be handled with great care when wrapping them in newspaper and when storing them (for a short time only!) in a well-marked paper bag.

Make sure that the ground is dry when searching for fossils in clay, because when wet, clay becomes plastic and smeary. If the ground starts to get wet while you are working in the field, it is easy to clean your tools and yourself if a stream is nearby. Rain also washes clay away, exposing pyrite fossils in the process. Fossil-rich clay or marl clay located on an open bank often displays beautiful pyrite fossils after a rain. In Germany, such fossil-collecting locations—a collector's paradise—are not easy to find. However, they are abundant in southern France,

with its large region in the south and west of the Cévennes Mountains known as *Terre Noire*, "black clay." In untouched locations, it is possible to gather a whole collection of fossils. Also, in Provence, many fossils embedded in the soft layers of the Lower Cretaceous period are washed out. Some pyrite fossils are preserved because of the influence of the sun, wind, and rain. Air and a lot of water change pyrite into iron oxide and sulfuric acid:

$$4\,FeS_2 \;+\; 15\,O_2 \;+\; 8\,H_2O \rightarrow$$
Pyrite $\qquad$ Oxygen $\qquad$ Water

$$2\,Fe_2O_3 \qquad + \qquad 8\,H_2SO_4$$
Iron oxide $\qquad\qquad$ Sulfuric acid

While some of the sulfuric acid is washed into the ground water, the remainder combines with iron oxide to become ferric sulfate (taking on the shape of a blossom). Pyrite fossils are often covered with a layer of iron oxide, either with yellowish-tinted iron ore, limonite, $FeO(OH)$, or with the brown-black hematite, Fe_2O_3, which looks like metal (15–3). These iron oxide layers are easily removed with a brass or bronze wire brush, which exposes surface markings for easier identification.

In general, pyrite fossils are the problem children of a fossil collection, since the sur-

Plate 11
1. A handful of shark teeth from Ursendorf from the upper marine deposits of the Tertiary period.
2. Raspberry-shaped bryozoan *Cellepora polytele* Reuss, 1⅜ inches wide (3 cm), from Ursendorf.
3. Sea-urchin *Spatangus desmaresti* Münster, 4 inches (10 cm) wide, also from the upper marine deposits near Ursendorf.

face, when exposed to warm, humid air, expands and can create not only sulfuric acid but also ferric sulfate deposits. A piece of wood covered with a brilliant layer of pyrite, found in Tertiary brown-coal deposits, will disintegrate into white powder and a yellow "sulfur-flower." Examples are the typical "blooming" of pyritic ammonites (15–4). The sulfuric acid that is released not only endangers the rest of the fossils in a collection, but also damages labels and the surrounding area. For this reason, it is important to remove the pieces that have been affected as soon as possible. Seal them properly and store them in a room with low humidity.

The beautifully shaped, but pyritized, sea lily stems (from Altenhagen near Bielefeld) that I have in my collection have changed very little over a period of some years, maybe because they have a more stable pyrite compound. I do not know of a foolproof protection against "blooming." I use a mixture of shellac and varnish. Sometimes I leave a particularly beautiful specimen untreated, using it as a test case, as well as a feast for the eye (15–5). When preserving a fossil, it is best to apply the shellac mixture to only one side, let this side dry, and then proceed with the other side.

It is not enough to "wash" pyrite fossils (alcohol works best) in order to remove clay crumbs. More often than not, it is necessary to use a mini-chisel, a dental explorer, or a fine needle in order to remove the hard clay particles that are baked into the grooves and lobes of a specimen (17–1). Chalklike deposits can be removed with acetic acid, which should be rinsed off thoroughly afterwards.

Whenever an ammonite undergoes rapid pyritization, the inner, chambered portion of the shell (phragmocone) can withstand the pressure that is created from clay sediments above much better than the animal's body chamber can. That space is often only recognizable as a rather unstable impression of the shell. (See Illus. 10 for cross-section of an ammonite.) Such a specimen can serve as a typical example in a large fossil collection (17–3). The pyritic portion should be cleaned with great care. Loose parts can be glued back on again.

Pyrite also grows in and around large organisms that are embedded in clay. I am not referring here to the 3-foot-tall (1 meter) pyritized sea lilies displayed in museums. (Those are rightfully admired as masterpieces for the work involved in their preparation.) Rather, I am thinking of specimens that are easy to find and to preserve, such as large ammonites. These might consist (on the outside, as well as the inside) of pyrite (17–2), or they might have a fossil-distorting pyrite coat (17–4).

Owning such a specimen gives a collector great pleasure. The amount of work required

Plate 12
1. Snails are carefully removed from a large piece of rock.
2. *Viviparus suevicus*, snails of up to 1½ inches (4 cm) in size, embedded in fine-grained sand near Kirchberg on the Iller.
3. Finished "plastic fossils" with *Viviparus*.
4. A sample with *Turritella turris* (Bastian) 2 inches (5 cm) long; upper marine deposits, from Ermingen near Ulm.

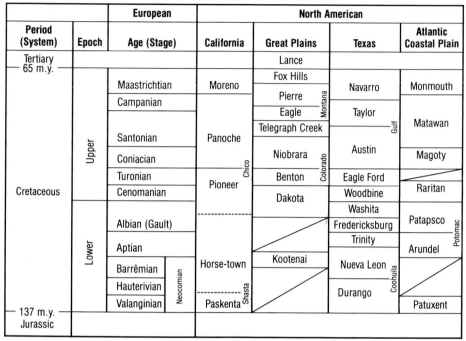

Table 4. Cretaceous Classification

		European	North American			
Period (System)	Epoch	Age (Stage)	California	Great Plains	Texas	Atlantic Coastal Plain
Tertiary — 65 m.y. —				Lance		
Cretaceous	Upper	Maastrichtian	Moreno	Fox Hills	Navarro	Monmouth
		Campanian	Panoche (Chico)	Pierre (Montana)	Taylor (Gulf)	Matawan
				Eagle (Montana)		
		Santonian	Panoche (Chico)	Telegraph Creek	Austin (Gulf)	Matawan
		Coniacian		Niobrara (Colorado)	Austin (Gulf)	Magoty
		Turonian	Pioneer (Chico)	Benton (Colorado)	Eagle Ford	
		Cenomanian	Pioneer (Chico)	Dakota	Woodbine	Raritan
	Lower	Albian (Gault)	Horse-town (Shasta)		Washita	Patapsco (Potomac)
					Fredericksburg	
		Aptian	Horse-town (Shasta)		Trinity	Arundel (Potomac)
		Barrêmian (Neocomian)	Horse-town (Shasta)	Kootenai	Nueva Leon (Coohuila)	
		Hauterivian (Neocomian)			Durango (Coohuila)	
		Valanginian (Neocomian)	Paskenta (Shasta)		Durango (Coohuila)	Patuxent
— 137 m.y. — Jurassic						

m.y. = millions (10^6) of years.

to prepare and preserve fossils is very satisfying, even if the finished product does not show the effort that went into the process. Only another collector will have some idea of the amount of deposits that had to be removed, the extent of the repairs that were necessary, of the sparks that went flying when a chisel was used, and the hydrogen sulfide fumes in your work area.

Exposing an embedded pyrite fossil is not very difficult when the clay is still damp, since it can easily be cut with a knife. The first step is to allow the fossil-bearing clay to dry out slowly, followed by cleaning it mechanically. Then apply shellac or any other appropriate spray to the specimen for preservation. Loose clay particles are best removed with a soft, small artist's brush, followed by an application of a fluosilicate waterproofing product to protect the clay. This will darken the clay and create a wonderful contrast to the glistening, golden fossil (18–1).

Sometimes only the shell of a large ammonite is pyritized. In that case, you might want to remove the clay from the fossil, piece by piece, even if some of the pyritized shell might be damaged in the process. What is left is a *steinkern* with a golden hue. In the opalescent clay from the Jurassic Aalenian stage (Dogger alpha), I once found an ammonite as large as the inside of my hand, with a massive pyrite center that had kept its original shape. In the same location, millions of other members of the species appeared only as compressed chalk deposits.

Many nonpyritized fossils are also present

Table 5.   Jurassic Classification

Period (System)	Epoch	European Age (Stage)	S. German Classification*	North America Wyoming Utah	North America Sierra Nevada
Cretaceous - 137 m.y.					
Jurassic	Malm = White Jurassic = Upper Jurassic	Purbeckian Portlandian	No comparable deposit		Knoxville
		Tithonian	ζ Zeta	Morrison	Mariposa
		Kimmeridgian	ε Epsilon / δ Delta / γ Gamma		
		Oxfordian	β Beta / α Alpha	Sundance	
	Dogger = Brown Jurassic = Middle Jurassic	Callovian .	ζ Zeta		Amador
		Bathonian	ε Epsilon	Gypsum Spring (Wyoming)	
		Bajocian	δ Delta / γ Gamma	Carmel (Utah)	Monte de Oro
		Aalenian	β Beta / α Alpha		Thompson
	Liassic = Black Jurassic = Lower Jurassic	Toarcian	ζ Zeta / ε Epsilon		Hardgrave
		Pliensbachian	δ Delta	Navajo	
			γ Gamma		
		Sinemurian	β Beta		Trail
			α₃ Alpha 3		
		Hettangian	α₂ Alpha 2 / α₁ Alpha 1	Kayenta	
- 195 m.y. Triassic					

*according to Quenstedt.   m.y. = millions of years (10^6 years).

in those clay layers that carry pyritized fossils, like belemnites (see Illus. 11), whose chamberlike portions are more often calcified than pyritized, and many smaller fossil remnants, mainly bivalves and snails. Fossils of a more robust structure can be harvested without inflicting much damage if the fossil-carrying clay is first allowed to dry out and then immersed in a water bath to wash off the clay deposits. Thin fossils, as well as small bivalve shells and snails, which would disintegrate when immersed in a water bath, can be freed from clay deposits with careful, successive dampening of the clay.

Fossils in Oil Shale Near Messel

Oil shale from the Messel region is unique. This becomes very clear when one is climbing, or rather, trying to climb, the black slate

rocks (which date from the Eocene some 50 million years ago) after a rainy day. Continuous slipping and sliding replaces progress. Maybe it is typical for this kind of slate that it can be cut with a knife. In dry weather, however, the material will start to flake and turn into dust. These observations say something about the difficulties collectors face in harvesting fossils from this material. In the past, stabilizing fossil remnants was only possible by covering them with a special lacquer—a problem geologists dealing with issues in brown-coal mining in Halle still struggle with to this day. Fish skeletons embedded in the oil-shale layers in Messel separate through the center. With some luck, each half of a separated shale piece contains one-half of the skeleton. A cast is prepared by pouring synthetic resin in the mold. After the resin has set, the outside of the skeleton is removed (19–2, 19–3). The result is an unprecedented preservation of the most minute fossil structures (8–1). Word got out among fossil collectors about these astounding results (even though the process seems so laborious) of preserving such fossils coming from a region that had been known for generations. In 1974, after much urgent advice from friends, I finally set out to look for these fish remnants in the oil-shale region near Messel. Since it was raining, it was easy to pack up the collected pieces in wet newspaper and plastic bags.

Back home, I began the process of preser-

Plate 13 (page 38)
1. Marl crumbs are removed, with the help of a brush.
2. Separating and lifting a piece of marl slate containing remnants of a plant.
3. Poplar leaf, 3⅛ inches long (8 cm), from Öhningen slate, upper freshwater deposits, near Radolfzell, where the organic matter has turned to coal.
4. Impression of the leaf from the underlying layer.

Plate 14 (page 40)
1. *Theodoxus crenulatus* (Klein), ¼ inch (7 mm), with a typical dotted shell, embedded in soft marl of the upper freshwater deposits from Pflummern near Riedling on Danube.
2. *Brotia escheri* Merian, 1½ inches (4 cm), from the same location and marl layer.
3. Ammonite *Androgynoceras maculatum* Young and Bird, 3⅛ inches (8 cm) and belemnite *Belemnites paxillosus*, 4 inches (10 cm), in marl from the Jurassic, Lower Pliensbachian stage (Liassic gamma).
4. A Miocene fish skeleton, 8 inches (20 cm), in light, very porous sediment near St. Bauzile, southern France.

Plate 15 (page 41)
1. A group of pyritized *Amaltheus* ammonites, up to 2⅜ inches (6 cm) in size, in a layer of clay from the Jurassic upper Pliensbachian stage (Liassic delta) near Göppingen.
2. Pyritized ammonite *Endemoceras*, 4¾ inches long (12 cm), with opalescent shell remnants in an almost vertical wall of clay from the Lower Cretaceous near Sarstedt, Hannover.
3. Pyritized ammonites from the Jurassic Toarcian stage (Upper Liassic), southern France, with a limonitic surface due to oxidation. Left: *Polyplectus*, 1½ inches (4 cm) long, in limonite; right: *Hildoceras*, 1⅜ inches (3.5 cm) in hematite.
4. A pyritized, "blooming" ammonite, 1½ inches (4 cm).
5. A pyritized *Echioceras*, 2 inches (5 cm), without a protective coat of shellac, from the Jurassic Sinemurian stage (Liassic beta), from the western Swabian Alps.

vation. I had only "word-of-mouth" instructions, but they yielded great results. What follows are those instructions, with a few additional tips.

1. I unwrapped and eventually joined the broken pieces, using a flat box filled with sand as a working surface (19–1). This enabled me to bring the fossil to a level position.

2. I filled in the cracks in the shale surrounding the skeleton with a paste made from ground-up shale shavings. Damage to the skeleton was repaired with a paste made from ground-up fish remnants (for instance, scales taken from those skeletons that I wanted to discard).

3. The material for the sandbox, built to exact measurements, was made from balsa wood, rather than from modeling clay or plaster of Paris.

4. Cracks in the wood and spaces between the wooden boards and the shale were carefully filled in with putty.

5. All parts of the fossil were dried with a hair dryer. I covered the fossil with damp cloths to prevent the shale from drying out. Clear lacquer, applied to the surface of the shale, will serve the same purpose.

6. I proceeded to remove all traces of oil with paint remover. After making sure that the surface and all the crevices had completely dried and all remaining particles had been removed, I covered the whole surface with a layer of epoxy, to which I added finely ground oil shale.

7. After the epoxy began to set, I covered the surface with a layer of Fiberglas and then added more epoxy until I had a thickness of at least ⅜ inch (1 cm) for a surface the size of 16 × 12 inches (40 × 30 cm).

8. After the epoxy had completely cured (24 hours later), I turned the box upside down and began to carefully remove all the oil shale.

9. With the help of water, brushes, and cleaning agents, I loosened and removed all remnants of the shale and all other particles or sediments from the fossil, using a dental drill and fine needles, where necessary, until the fish skeleton was completely exposed.

10. Those portions of the plate that did not include the fossil showed all the structure and characteristics of the original oil-shale plate. Thanks to the ground-up shale I had added to the epoxy (19–2), those portions even had the proper color. It was not necessary to add any other coloring agent to the clear epoxy (19–3). Mixing the epoxy with ground-up shale has an additional advantage: a mistake made in the course of cleanup will not be noticed.

Plate 16
Pyritized portions of sea lily stems, 3⅛ inches long (8 cm), from the Jurassic Middle Liassic near Altenhagen/Bielefeld.

11. Finally, all edges and corners were sanded, and the back of the cast was covered with an adhesive, velvety film.

12. Such a "fossil plate" (64–4) can easily be displayed on a wall without a frame (see also Illus. 39).

I am certain that the procedure described above will undergo many improvements. Messel has become known the world over for the number and excellent condition of the rare fossils dating from the Eocene, which are vivid testimony to the stages of mammal evolution. All fossils found there are being preserved by professionals in a fashion similar to the one described above. It is my hope that the area will remain available for future paleontological research.

Fossils located in brown-coal deposits at the Geiseltal (Geisel Valley) and the oil-shale layers near Messel are difficult to collect and to prepare because of the unstable, high moisture content of the deposits. Older, more hardened oil-shale deposits, such as the Poseidon Shale (Jurassic Period) or Bundenbach Shale (Devonian) contain correspondingly more stable fossils, which makes the work much easier.

Fossils Embedded in Hard Deposits

Calcified Fossils Embedded in Limestone

Those who hike the Jura Mountains—for example, the Swiss Jura, which gave its name to the Jurassic period, or the Swabian and

Plate 17 (page 44)
1. Hardened clay is embedded in the crevices of this 2⅜-inch (6-cm) long *Oxynoticeras oxynotum* (Quenstedt) from the Jurassic Sinemurian stage (Liassic beta) from Schömberg near Balingen.
2. *Teloceras*, a pyritized ammonite, 10 inches (25 cm) wide, was discovered and preserved.
3. *Echioceras* from the Jurassic Sinemurian (Liassic beta) near Sunthausen, with a pyritized phragmocone, and a flattened, nonpyritized body chamber; overall size 2⅜ inches (6 cm).
4. *Amaltheus gibbosus* (Schlotheim), 2 inches (5 cm) long, only partially pyritized, an ammonite from the Jurassic upper Pliensbachian (Liassic delta), from Reichenbach near Aalen.
5. Large, 8¾-inch (22 cm), pyritized *Teleoceras blagdeni* (Sowerby) from the Jurassic Bajocian stage (Dogger delta) from Beuren near Kirchheim.

Plate 18 (page 46)
1. *Echioceras*, ¾ inch (2 cm), on black clay.
2. Pyritized belemnite phragmocone, 2 inches (5 cm), from the Liassic in Osterkappeln near Osnabrück.
3. Untouched *Pleurotomaria* snail, ½ inch (1.5 cm) across, in clay from the Jurassic upper Pliensbachian stage (Liassic delta), from Marloffstein, Franconian Jura Mountains.

Plate 19 (page 47)
1. Preparation to make a synthetic resin cast of an oil-shale plate from Messel (with sandbox).
2. Surface characteristics and color of the oil shale, as well as of the fish, *Amia kehreri*, 10 inches (25 cm), are well preserved.
3. *Amphiperca multiformis*, a large, 7⅛-inch (18-cm) perch, from Messel, embedded in clear synthetic resin.

Franconian Alps in southern Germany—will find calcified fossils every step of the way: in road banks, as rock layers, on steep slopes that give the landscape its typical character, and—most of all—in large and small rock quarries in the yellowish-white or weatherbeaten gray limestone. Almost without fail, it is here that a collector will find an abundant amount of fossils. In England, the Portland Stone from the middle Tithonian period, frequently used in construction, is comparable.

Fossil collectors usually concentrate on a location where the limestone has already begun to deteriorate (20–3). Calcified fossils in hard limestone are difficult to remove, since both the fossils and the limestone are hard. Even cracks and fissures in the stone are not helpful; the fossils will break into pieces. On the other hand, weatherbeaten limestone will separate much more easily from the surface of a fossil. Gentle tapping with a hammer frees bivalves and ammonites (20–1). Excavating fossils from limestone from the Tertiary period, which has not hardened quite as much, is particularly satisfying. Such limestone often contains beautiful snail shells that do not need any further preparation (3–2). Sometimes the bitumen present in porous limestone has formed a black coating on the surface of the fossils (20–2). If the limestone is very hard, the fossil may be totally black.

Now, back to the hypothetical fossil collectors hiking through the Jura Mountains. On a fossil hunt in the spring, they are looking for fossils below fossil-carrying limestone slopes. Of course, they do this only in the absence of wind and after taking proper precautions, such as wearing protective helmets. They will most likely find many brachiopods, like terebratulids and rhynchonellidids (21–1), but they also may find small ammonites and even sea-urchins, in condition that do not require any further preparation (21–2).

It is a long way from the moment that a calcified fossil is discovered, to its successful extraction from the limestone (intact, we hope), and until it is ready to be added to a collection or exhibition. Fossils whose outlines are only partially visible in limestone, or in layers of limestone, will be a problem for the collector, if the fossils are embedded in a rock stratum from which they cannot be extracted or which cannot be broken up. requires a great deal of strength to make a sufficiently deep groove around the fossil to cut it out. The collector has to be prepared, particularly when the rock is relatively "new," for the fossil to break. Usually the effort to extract such a fossil is only worthwhile if the collector can make certain that the underside of the fossil is in good shape. Often, the exposed surface of the specimen has been damaged over time by water and

Plate 20

1. Ammonite *Coroniceras rotiformis* (Sowerby), 10 inches (25 cm) wide, extracted from a weathered rock from the Jurassic Sinemurian stage (Liassic alpha) near the Wutach region.
2. Shell, 1⅜ inches (3 cm) wide of a *Coretus cornu* (Brogniart), a snail from the lower freshwater deposits near Ehingen, is dark-colored due to its exposure to bitumen.
3. Fossil collectors working at a site from the White Jurassic period near Unterhausen/Danube (now off limits).

other influences, while the underside has remained protected. This holds true for many fossils, even if they have been embedded under different circumstances.

Searching for and collecting fossils in undisturbed locations is wonderful, but fossil collectors should not ignore places where construction crews have deposited the earth they have excavated. In such locations, collectors can be certain not to interfere with anybody and often will find layers of rocks ideally spread out in front of them. Limestone plates that are hard, but not too thick, can be broken up into smaller, transportable pieces—ideally, without damaging the fossils they contain—and can be worked at home in peace and quiet.

In North America, some of the best-preserved trilobites can be found in limestone deposits—for instance, from the Ordovician Blackriverian period in the Criner Hills, Carter County, Oklahoma, and in the violet limestone of the Arbuckle Mountains; and from the Ordovician Trentonian period near Sulfur, Oklahoma. Beautiful and rare trilobites also have been found in the limestone of the Silurian Cayugan, in Lowrence Uplift, near Ada, Oklahoma. Exceptionally well-preserved trilobites also come from the Joliet Dolomites (Silurian Niagaran) near Grafton, Illinois, and from the same period, from deposits in Waldron Shale in Tennessee.

Silicified Fossils in Limestone

Limestone deposits in northern German contain many silicified fossils (see the sec tion "Fossils in Limestone Layers"). Man such fossils can be found in open fields in th fall in the White Jurassic deposits in souther Germany, particularly in the vicinity c Heidenheim and Urach. The deposits in th vicinity of Nattheim contain many typica specimens of silicified fossils. They can usu ally be found in pieces of limestone on con struction sites. Because of silicification these deposits contain weathered fossils an remnants of corals. Suitable pieces can b taken home and soaked in dilute acetic aci (after you have tested one sample), whic will remove the limestone from the fossil This process has yielded beautiful speci mens, whole groups of fossils and coral (40–2), from which we have at least 10 different types—sea-urchins, brachiopod (8–2), bivalves, sponges, and other remnant of organisms from the ocean of the Uppe White Jurassic Kimmeridgian stage, datin back some 140 million years. In the Unite States, silicified fossils are found near Lak Huron in deposits from the Niagara group o the Middle Silurian period.

It is important that the acetic acid be di luted to 10–15% to avoid the destruction o delicate fossil structures. To protect the deli cate surfaces of sea-urchins, bivalves, an

Plate 21
1. Large rhynchonellids *Cymatorhynchia quadriplicata* Zeiten, 1¾ inches (4.5 cm), brachiopod from layers of the Dogger period, from Normandy.
2. Sea-urchin *Plegiocidaris coronata* (Goldfuss), 1⅛ inches (3 cm), from marl chalk of the Uppe White Jurassic from Nollhof near Sigmaringen.

brachiopods from the damaging effects of the acid as you work, the cleaning process should be interrupted periodically, the specimen removed, washed, dried and any exposed fossil should be covered with a layer of wax. Eyes and hands should be protected with goggles and rubber gloves. See the safety section in the "Preparation" chapter for further information.

Not all of the limestone deposits on silicified fossils should be removed. A coral that has been broken open often displays wonderful quartz crystals that remain unaffected by the acid treatment. These beautiful mountain crystals are remains from the primeval world. Pieces from primeval ocean floors contain numerous silicified fossils that have only been partially freed from the deposits surrounding them (23). These provide fascinating evidence of how layer after layer of deposits developed over millions of years.

Fossils Embedded in Flat Layers

Fossils Embedded in Limestone Layers

Whenever limestone is discussed we talk (at least in German-speaking regions) about Solnhofen and its limestone deposits. The area is famous for the discovery of *Archaeopteryx*, the oldest known, primeval bird. The limestone deposits are located in the Altmühl Valley in Bavaria between the towns of Weissenburg and Eichstätt, and in the foothills of Kelheim. Limestone can also be found in other locations and from other time periods, such as the deposits from the Eocene in Bolca in northern Italy, and the fossil-rich Tertiary deposits (already known at the beginning of the 18th century) from the stone quarries in Öhningen north of Wangern at the Schienberg near Lake Constance.

In the United States, world-famous fossils of freshwater fish are present in "slabby limestone" from the lower Eocene period (see Plate 25) in the Green River Formation in Wyoming, Utah, and Colorado. Perfectly preserved trilobites (see Plates 10 and 41) are found in very hard, but fine-grained layers of limestone deposits from the Cambrian Wheeler Formation, in Millard County, Utah. Collectors report fossil finds in limestone deposits in Driftwood Creek, near Smithers, British Columbia, Canada. They have found wonderfully preserved leaves (sequoia) and insects (mosquitoes) from the Tertiary Eocene to the Oligocene periods.

"Young" limestone deposits are not as easily separated as those that have been found exposed on slopes and are already weatherbeaten. At the limestone quarries

Plate 22
1. A large (8-inch or 20-cm) ammonite, still enclosed in rock, is carefully exposed.
2. A ceratite (a type of ammonite), found in upper shell limestone, 4¾ inches (12 cm), before preparation.
3. The same ceratite after preparation.
4–6. A *Leioceras comptum* (Reinecke), 4¾ inches (12 cm), found in the chamoisite oolite of the Jurassic Dogger Beta (Aalenian stage). **4.** With the shell intact. **5.** Exposed. **6.** Chemically treated.

in Ohningen (only kept open for fossil-collecting purposes), limestone left exposed to the elements during the winter was much easier to handle in the spring. The quarries in Öhningen do not exist anymore—they were buried by mud slides and are now covered with vegetation. Plate 24–1 shows a piece from that location that I dragged out of a foxhole.

However, in the Altmühl valley, we still have layers and layers of limestone, stacked on top of each other over generations. This is the place where old printing blocks and scraps from tile production were discarded. With patience and diligence, the collector can break open weathered pieces of limestone and literally leaf through the pages of the earth's history.

Floating sea lilies (24–3) and wormlike specimens are part of the earliest discoveries. Next came small-boned fish (54–4) and flattened ammonites (24–2).

Limestone blocks ought to be taken home before being cut into proper sizes. It is much easier to work with pliers and stone saws at home. Many a precious limestone specimen has been destroyed during transport, because the very thin, weathered layers break so easily. It is advisable to wrap limestone pieces in lots of newspaper, with layers of foam in between for added protection. I usually protect valuable pieces with foam and then pack them between two pieces of cardboard

(26–1). Extracting fossils from limestone is *the* test of a collector's patience. Luckily, most finds need no preparation besides proper shaping. At most, the finished plates are sprayed with a clear lacquer or fixative (which should be sprayed on from the proper distance if applied as a spray), which binds the delicate chalky surface, providing a more stable one (see the chapter on preparation for more information).

It takes a passionate fossil collector to find traces of a flying dinosaur in limestone quarries. Usually they are discovered in the cross-sections of limestone plates. The expert will assemble the pieces that most likely contain a fossil. With the help of a scraping knife, a fine-tipped needle, and magnifying glasses, he or she will then set out to carefully remove the chalk from the fossil. Practical experience and knowledge gained from reading literature and journals are very helpful in recognizing fossils and in anticipating their actual positions. This is not a job for the average collector, who should ask for help at the nearest geological institute. However, the amateur may want to attempt the preparation of the remnants of bony fish (58–2) or aptychi, part of the jaw of an ammonite.

The waterbug *Mesobelostomum* (26–2, 26–3), 2 inches (5 cm) in length, including its antlers, gives a typical picture of a limestone fossil. The positive part is located on the bottom plate, while the remainder of the

Plate 23
Fossils from the Nattenheim region are silicified, making it possible, with the help of acid, to expose fossils from a larger, 6⅜-inch (16 cm) section of limestone This is a sample of a primeval ocean floor.

fossil has formed a cavity on the other half of the plate. This shows that the organism was embedded while on its back. The collector who not only works diligently on separating the layers of limestone but also pauses to observe the surface will be able perhaps to detect a starfish, or the very faint traces of an arthropod (most likely the remnants of the shedding process). These remnants can be clearly seen with the help of ultraviolet light.

In the last couple of years, collectors have discovered plant fossils in certain layers of limestone (27–3, 27–4). Identification without the help of good literature or professional advice is very difficult.

Reddish iron and black manganese oxide enter rocks in liquid form through cracks and often crystalize around fossils, creating delightful shapes in limestone plates (1–4).

Fossils in Shale

It is very difficult for an amateur fossil collector to distinguish among the different combinations of limestone and clay while on location, which produce different types of marl (see Table 3). For that reason, the collector distinguishes them according to their degree of hardness. Hard shale may develop when clay sediments have been deposited evenly and, through tectonic events, they have been changed into thin, layered, clayish shale, such as the shale mountains in the Rhine Valley.

The shale from the Swabian Alps is much valued by the fossil collector, because gold-shimmering ammonite molds are found in huge numbers in some layers of shale from the Black Jurassic epsilon (Toarcian stage) (28–2). Paper-thin compressed fossils are

Plate 24 (page 56)

1. Limestone, 8 inches thick (20 cm), from the Miocene period near Öhningen, shows parallel layers that are easier to work with after they have undergone weathering.
2. Positive and negative of a typically compressed ammonite embedded in limestone near Solnhofen, from the Jurassic Tithonian stage (Malm zeta).
3. A fossil frequently found in limestone: *Saccocoma pectinata* (Goldfuss), a floating sea lily, 1½ inches (4 cm) long.
4. A bony fish, 10 inches (25 cm) long, in a limestone plate. A fine needle and a knife were used to unearth this specimen.

Plate 25 (page 58)

1. This beautiful small fish, *Knightia alta*, up to 2⅜ inches (6 cm) in length, dates from the Eocene period; it is from the Green River Formation in Wyoming.
2. The central axis of this bryozoan colony, *Archimedes*, in a stone plate 4 inches (10 cm) wide, looks like a drill bit. It dates from the Carboniferous-Mississippian period and comes from Floraville, Illinois.

Plate 26 (page 59)

1. Fossils embedded in limestone plates should be protected by wrapping them between two pieces of rigid cardboard.
2. and 3. This waterbug, *Mesobelostomum*, 2 inches long (5 cm), including antlers, is a rare find. It is from limestone plates near Eichsätt. The mold (3) on the right plate shows the fossil's remnants with the bug belly-up. The left plate (2) is the cast.

usually exposed, and the collector does not need to use a needle or scraper to remove the shale (29–1). To avoid oxidation, gold-colored ammonites should be protected the same day they are excavated. A solution made from shellac and lacquer—or any other similar product—will delay deterioration of pyrite. Even experts do not know of a 100% safe way to protect pyrite, other than removing all moisture and enclosing it in an airtight space. Even those pyritized specimens displayed in museums have been known to fall apart after 30 years in spite of all the protective measures employed. Gray shale, when treated with soluble fluosilicates to waterproof it, changes to a deep black, creating a striking contrast to the color of the fossil.

The attentive fossil collector can also find other fossils in shale. Perhaps he will locate calcified belemnites, the cuttlefish *Geoteuthis bollensis* (29–2), or petrified wood (28–1).

If necessary, fossils embedded in shale can be excavated with the help of a needle and knife. The fossils must be protected from dampness and humidity. Tectonic pressure has compressed fossils to one-tenth of their original thickness in some shale deposits, like the fish from the Lower Permian period (54–1, 54–2). The most beautiful and best preserved fossils are from the Devonian period near Bundenbach/Hunsrück. Working

with needles and the most delicate scraping knives, expert fossil collectors were able to prepare these beautiful fossils.

Some fossils from the Devonian oceans, often recognizable only by faint irregularities in the rock layer covering them, are found in excellent condition. Portions of the organisms have been preserved in minute detail due to an extremely thin coating of pyritic and silicic acid. Preparing such specimens is difficult, and only a little less so if the position of the fossil has been determined by an X ray. In addition to X rays, geological laboratories use sandblasting to free fossils from the deposits surrounding them. The use of bronze wire brushes is rejected because of the damage they cause to the delicate structure of the fossil. Advice on how to best prepare these fossils is available in specialized literature.

A fossil from Hunsrück Shale, prepared with a brass-wire brush, was given to me by a fossil collector (29–4). A brass-wire brush will not leave a metallic shine on the surface of the fossil, which happens when a bronze wire brush is used, even in the absence of pyritization. It seems that no chemical solutions have been developed to assist in this preparation process; even hot-and-cold treatment (discussed in the chapter on preparation) is not helpful. Therefore, what is left for the removal of deposits is tedious work with

Plate 27
1. A brittle star, *Geocoma carinata* (Goldfuss), 2⅜ inches (6 cm).
2. A trace of the discarded skin and legs of a young crab in a limestone plate near Langenaltheim.
3. and **4**. In general, plant remains are difficult to identify; fossil collectors are always looking for relevant literature. Left plant is 3½ inches (9 cm) long; the width of the stem of the right plant is ½ inch (1.5 cm).

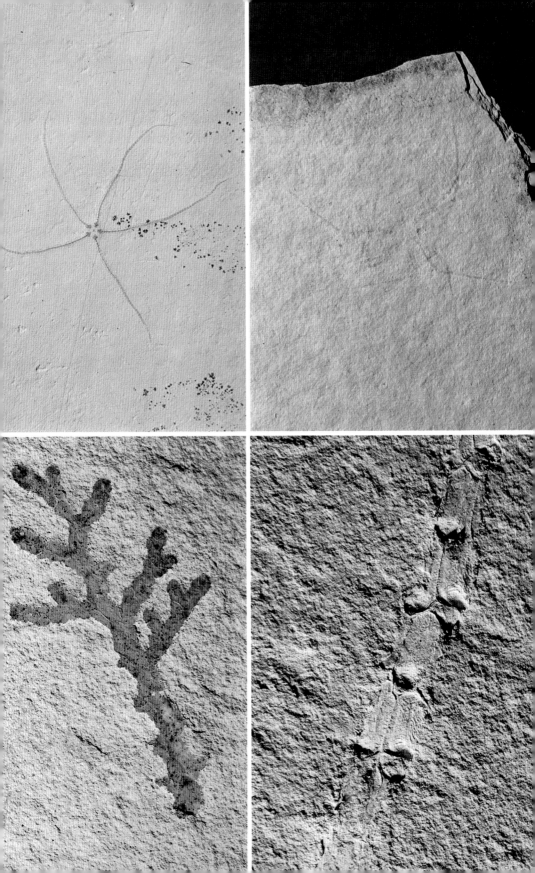

needles, sharp knives, concentration on the part of the collector, and a steady hand—and surely a good portion of luck!

In the United States, shale-clay deposits (a combination of clay, rock, fine sand, and volcanic materials) from the Pierre Shale of the Upper Cretaceous period (Campanian and Maastrichtian stages, see Table 4) are found whole, particularly in Colorado (Pueblo County) and Wyoming (Red Bird and Wasta), and also in Montana and in western South Dakota. The fossils in these locations have retained their shapes. The aragonitic ammonite shells have mostly changed to calcite and even to agate. The most beautiful fossils are embedded in limestone concretions. Wherever the shell has been removed or has broken off, wonderful branched lobe lines are visible on the surface of the ammonite *steinkern* (47). Fossils found in some locations still have aragonitic mother-of-pearl shells (47).

In soft slate-clay deposits (graptolite slate) from the Ordovician Chazyan period in the eastern United States, near Saginaw, Alabama, one can find some very rare types of trilobites in the Athens Formation. However, they are not as well preserved as those in the limestone deposits further west.

Fossils in Plant Shale from the Carboniferous Period

Subtropical environments, regions near shorelines, and areas with high humidity provided the right conditions for plant life to change into coal during the Carboniferous period. Recognizable remnants of plants are seldom found in coal deposits. The actual cell structures have changed into coal. However, in some coal deposits one can find peat dolomite, pieces of dolomite that contain fossilized remnants of plants. Plant remains can be identified by cutting a section of the sample and using color to tint the material. The fossil collector should look for plant remains in slag heaps where plant shale is most easily found. It is here that impressions typical for such plant remnants, from the bark of *Lepidodrendron* and *Sigillaria*, can be found (30–1, 30–2). Other three-dimensional remains may be found, like the *steinkern* of a calamite (paleozoic fossil plant) or the delicate impression of a fern leaf (30–3, 30–4). Examples of these are the productive Coal Measures from the Upper Pennsylvanian period in Appalachian locations, as well as comparable deposits in middle England and Scotland. These specimens need little preparation. Coal residue should be removed from the bark structure with a fine needle. Identifying such specimens is also lots of fun. Good literature and wonderful museum exhibits are available to give the collector a hand.

Fossils Embedded in Plant Shale from the Maar Near Randeck

Fossil-rich deposits embedded in a combination of hard, thin-layered shale with lime-

Plate 28
1. Two pieces of amber jet coal, formed from wood. Above: 6 inches wide (15 cm), with barite veins in between. Below: shiny-black amber jet coal from shale deposits.
2. In search of fossils in Poseidon Shale from the Jurassic Toarcian stage (Liassic epsilon), in the Swabian Alps.

stone and silicified remnants of lava that contain plant remains (65–3) and insects offer the fossil collector in the Maar, at the northern edge of the Swabian Alps, a unique picture of the world as it existed about 10 to 15 million years ago, during the Sarmatian stage of the Tertiary period (see Table 2).

It is difficult to split these hard layers evenly. One tip promising success is to heat the plate of rocks in the oven and cool them off immediately in cold water. This method can also be used when working with similar shale plates from other locations.

Fossils in Layers of Oolitic Rock

Water-soluble substances often attach themselves to small particles during the process of crystallization, forming small beads or globules called *oolites*. The subsequent rock that is created in such a way is also called an oolite. We have:

Iron oolite from brown or red ironstone oolites;

Silicic oolite from limestone oolites, bonded by silicic acid;

Roe stone from limestone oolites cemented together by sand;

Pea-shaped stones from aragonite oolites, cemented together by lime.

Typical oolites in England come from Jurassic deposits, the Inferior Oolite (Aalenian–Middle Bajocian) and the Great Oolite (Upper Bajocian–Lower Bathonian).

Plate 29 (page 64)
1. Shell bivalve *Steinmannia bronnii* (Voltz), up to ⅜ inch wide (1 cm), previously called *Posidonia bronnii*, covering individual rock layers in huge amounts and giving the Poseidon Shale its name.
2. This cuttlefish, *Geoteuthis bollensis* (Zieten), (6⅜ inches or 16 cm) now called *Belopeltis aalensis*, with its hornlike covering, was preserved, still showing the indentations and remnants of its ink bladder.
3. The ammonite *Lytoceras fimbriatum* (Zieten), 5⅜ inches wide (13 cm), stands out well against the fluosilicate-treated surface of the shale.
4. Head and tail plate of a trilobite, 2 inches long (5 cm), *Phacops*, from the Devonian Hunsruck Shale near Bundenbach. These might possibly be remnants of its cuticle, since both parts are positioned next to each other, but not originally attached.

Plate 30 (page 66)
Plants from the Carboniferous period:
1. Impression of the bark from a *Lepidodendron* with leaf stigmata, 1 inch (2.5 cm), Westphalian C, Ibbenbüren.
2. Impressions of the bark of a *Sigillaria* with ⅜-inch-wide (1 cm), vertically arranged leaf stigmata, Westphalian stage C, Ibbenbüren.
3. Portion of the trunk of a calamite, 4 inches (10 cm) wide, with internodes between two leaf nodules (stigmata), Westphalian stage C, Ibbenbüren.
4. Frond, 2¾ × 3⅛ inches (7 × 8 cm) from a tree fern, *Pecopteris*, Westphalian stage D, Piesberg.

Plate 31 (page 67)
1. A barely visible ammonite, *Macrocephalites*, 6 inches wide (15 cm), embedded in iron oolite, from the Jurassic Callovian stage (Dogger zeta).
2. *Macrocephalites macrocephalus* Schlotheim, 6 inches (15 cm) wide, from Albstadt, Swabian Alps.
3. *Parkinsonia parkinsoni* Sowerby, 2⅜ inches (6 cm), from the Jurassic Bathonian stage (Dogger delta), near Sengenthal, Lower Palatinate, during the first stage of preparation.
4. *Parkinsonia*, 2⅜ inches (6 cm), preparation completed.

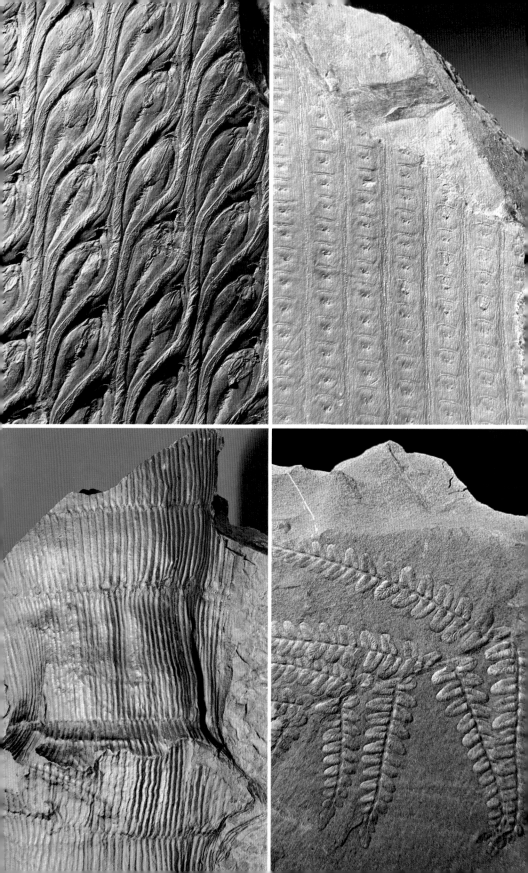

I will discuss first fossils that are embedded in iron oolites. Rock layers containing iron give the Brown Jurassic its name, because the majority of its rock layers are brown. Abandoned iron-ore mines are a good place to find iron oolites in fossil-rich rock layers. Often embedded in hard rocks, fossils can be freed from the iron-bearing oolites with a chisel, a needle, and knives. Classic examples are the fossils found near Sengenthal/Oberpfalz from the Jurassic Middle Dogger. Hardly noticeable in the rock, these ammonites can be prepared so that they look as if they were created from manmade materials (31).

Iron oolite layers from the Middle Dogger also contain giant belemnites (32–3), extinct cephalopods, whose pieces, if broken, can be joined together again (48–3). The fossil collector can carefully excavate large remnants of a belemnite, gently lift the fossil, piece by piece, and wrap it in newspaper (32–1, 32–2). The collector should mark on each piece an identifying number indicating where it belongs, with a sketch to go with it, and pack everything in a carton, making sure that nothing gets lost.

In 1977, during the construction of a reservoir, fossil collectors were able to excavate ammonites from the iron-bearing rock layers of the Jurassic Dogger gamma (Bajocian stage) near Nenningen. Some specimens were 18 inches (45 cm) wide and could be restored all the way into their interior volutions (32–4).

In the rock layers of the Brown Jurassic beta (Aalenian stage), the fossil collector will learn how different the deposits can be. While he or she will find iron-ore-bearing brown-red oolites near Aalen and Wasseralfingen on the east side of the Swabian Alps, on the west side near Blumberg, the collector will find greenish-gray iron oolites (32–5). The latter are a little more difficult to extract because the rock is so hard. However, the effort with hammer, chisel, knife, needle, and glue is often rewarded with particularly beautiful specimens, enriching any collection (22–4, 22–5, 22–6).

Fossils in Concretions

"Concretion" comes from the Latin "concretio," meaning *accumulation*. The accumulation of minerals within a rock deposit usually starts with organic substances at the core, growing from the inside out. Fossil collectors also speak of nodules or geodes (from the Greek word *geodes*, meaning *earthlike*). Although concretion and geode mean the same thing, we distinguish between different types of concretion, for instance: clay, limestone, clay-iron ore, pyrite, marcasite, sandstone, and flint or quartz. In the United States, worm and plant fossils (in

Plate 32
1. Extracting a large belemnite, 18 inches long (45 cm), from the Jurassic Dogger delta level near Bopfingen.
2. Individual pieces are carefully wrapped and packed.
3. *Megateuthis giganteus* (Schlotheim), a 14-inch (35-cm) belemnite from Bopfingen, glued together.
4. *Sonninia tessoniana* D'Orbigny, 18 inches wide (45 cm), from the Jurassic Bajocian stage (Dogger gamma), from Nenningen, Swabian Alps.
5. A 3-inch (7 cm) ichthyosaur vertebra from a chamoisite oolite from the Jurassic Aalenian stage (Dogger beta) in the Wutach region.

siderite concretions) from the Carboniferous period can be found in the Francis Creek Shale near Essex, Pennsylvania (7). Wonderful ammonites were embedded in limestone concretions from the Fox Hills Formation in South Dakota (47, 48). The ammonites' hard, white, sometimes opalized shells often break when the concretion is opened up. If the shell remnants are removed, very attractive lobelines become visible. In England, fossil-rich geodes from the Jurassic Pliensbachian stage (Dogger), and from the Toarcian period are found in Whitby, Yorkshire (Yorkshire Nodules).

Every fossil collector ought to examine concretions very carefully, because they often contain well-preserved fossils. Often the shape serves as a clue as to the type of fossil it is; for instance, a crab fossil (33–1), or a fish, or remnants of ammonites are protruding. We do not have one single recipe for opening a concretion. In general, the hot–cold treatment (see the chapter on preparation) is the first step for separating the deposits from the fossil. This is followed by gentle taps with a hammer. It is a matter of experience as to where to apply the taps, since concretions differ in shape, type, and content. A crab embedded in a limestone concretion must be handled with special care (33–2). It may be impossible to extract a crab fossil if it is surrounded by tough pyrite deposits.

Pyritized ammonites embedded in clay contain clay nodules that also develop from the inside out (34–1). These are similar to the clay-iron ore nodules from the Lower, Red-Layered Permian period near Lebach, which contain coprolites (fossil excrement) of reptiles (34–3). Clay nodules and limestone nodules from Unterstürmig are easier to open (34–4). Chalk deposits surrounding ammonites can be brushed off, often surprising fossil collectors with a beautifully calcified *steinkern* inside.

Organic remnants are also the source of concretions and crystal formations in sandy deposits. In 1975, working near the town of Ochsenhausen/Biberach, I came across very romantic-looking crystal formations (34–2) in the sand of the upper freshwater deposits. I also found individual sand-crystal roses and calcified sand crystals, which originated as fossilized remnants of trees (35).

Pyrite concretions are often impressively enhanced by their crystal sheen (36–2). Clay deposits are removed with the help of a chisel and a fine needle. The fossil collector might also use dilute acid (see the chapter on preparation for safety information on acids).

Flint nodules have been found in deposits from the Cretaceous period that, in northern Germany, often identify the boundary of the Iron Age. These nodules contain hardened fossils that are embedded in chalcedony, jas-

Plate 33

1. A crustacean in a 5¼-inch (14-cm) concretion that shows only a faint outline of its shape.
2. A 4¾-inch (12-cm) crustacean, *Antrimpos kiliani*, without antennae, in an opened limestone nodule from the Jurassic Callovian (Upper Dogger) near La Voulte, southern France.

per, and opal, or, with their amorphous, non-crystallized quartz, surround fossils that have been stabilized by silicic acid (6–4). In the United States a 39-inch (1 meter) long concretions of slatelike clay rocks, exposed through weathering, can be found near Havre, Montana.

Locations Where Fossils Accumulate

The way bivalves and snail shells accumulate along the seashore today is not different than the way remnants of animals were embedded in great numbers millions of years ago. Of course, the exact locations were not necessarily influenced by ocean currents or overpopulation. Many factors contributed to an accumulation. Washed together in huge numbers, remnants of organisms were embedded far away from the locations where they originally lived. Many fossil collectors are astounded when they encounter layers of deposits, often several meters thick, in the Black Jurassic alpha 3 (Lower Sinemurian stage) that developed through the fossilization of the oyster *Gryphaea arcuata*. Collectors will, no doubt, take one of these specimens home for their collection (36–1). They will also find other fossils: thick layers of snail shells embedded in sandstone from the Liassic alpha 2 (Hettangian stage), and also the remnants of stems of sea lilies that are embedded in the mussel-shell limestone from the Triassic period (37–1).

Much more visible, but also requiring more preparation, are belemnite, ammonite, and snail shell accumulations (37–2, 37–3), which often make a collection particularly attractive. Freshly damp deposits from the Tertiary, in Upper Swabia, with billions of small *Dreissensia* shells (37–4, 37–5), are an example of such accumulations still hiding in the earth.

Fossils in Amber

The most famous amber is from the Baltic. Amber's chemical formula is $C_{10}H_{16}O$. Because it is predominantly a product of the pine tree *Pinus succinifera*, it is also called *succinite*. In Europe, fossilized plant resin probably developed during the later Eocene, about 40 million years ago. Later, it was incorporated in the blue deposits of the Oligocene period and washed up on the eastern Baltic shores. Amber is found in many different places around the globe in deposits from the Carboniferous period. Remnants of plant resin from a later period (about 1 million years ago) are called *copal*.

Fossils embedded in clear amber show in

Plate 34

1. Clay concretion on an ammonite, *Schotheimia angulata* Schlotheim, 2⅜ inches wide (6 cm), from Buer near Osnabrück.
2. Duckling, a sand concretion, 4⅜ inches tall (11 cm), with sand crystals that have been polished by moving water, from the Tertiary upper freshwater deposits near Ochsenhausen/Upper Swabia.
3. Clay–ironstone concretion, 6 inches wide (15 cm). A deformed coprolite is embedded. From deposits near Lebach from the red-layered Lower Permian period.
4. Ammonite *Pleuroceras spinatum* Bruguiere, 2¾ inches (7 cm), with a chalklike, white shell, embedded in limestone concretion.

detail up to more than 1/1000 of a millimeter the exterior shapes of the animals within, even though the inside is nothing more than an empty cavity. The embedded animal remnants are mostly those of insects, spiders, and mites (38).

Amber is found in many different locations. Dieter Schlee and Werner Glöckner have published a list of every well-known location on the globe in the eighth edition of the journal *Stuttgarter Beiträge zu Naturkunde* [Contributions to Natural Science from Stuttgart].* In addition to the already mentioned location on the shores of the Baltic Sea, they list ones in Haiti from the Oligocene period (Dominican amber) and those contained in the layers of the Lower

---

*Book 8, Staatl. Museum f. Naturkunde, Stuttgart, Germany, 1978.

Chalk stage in the Lebanon Mountains, the oldest known fossil-containing amber.

In many cases, the rough surface and cracks prevent a view of the inside of a specimen. Amber can be made more transparent if it is immersed in a clear, oily solution of benzoin, $C_{14}H_{12}O_2$, a solution to be handled with care in a well-ventilated room or outdoors since its fumes can cause difficulty in swallowing.

If amber is left exposed to air and light over decades, it will turn garnet red. Several methods exist to lighten the color of amber. When exposed to strong ultraviolet rays, amber turns into a white powder. Amber from Lebanon is usually very brittle. Scientific studies can only be undertaken after this amber has been treated with a coat of resin (e.g., polyester resin) and the coating has been carefully sanded—first with a rough, and then with a fine sandpaper—and then finely polished with a sandpaper of 800 grit.

Plate 35 (page 74)
Calcified sand crystals, 2 inches (5 cm) long, extending from a fossilized tree remnant, found in the sands of the upper freshwater deposits in Ochsenhausen near Biberach, Upper Swabia.

Plate 36 (page 76)
1. Rock-forming oysters *Gryphaea arcuata* Lamarck, 2 to 2¾ inches long (5 to 7 cm), from the Jurassic Sinemurian stage (Liassic alpha 3) near Schwäbisch Gmünd.
2. Almost totally embedded in pyrite concretion, the ammonite *Pleuroceras reichenbachense* Schlegelmilch, 1¼ inches (3.5 cm) wide.

Plate 37 (page 77)
1. Remnants, up to 2¾ inches (7 cm) in diameter, of the sea lily *Encrinus liliiformis* Lamarck, in shell limestone near Crailsheim.
2. Accumulation of ammonites, 4 inches (10 cm), including *Pleuroceras*, from the Upper Pliensbachian (Liassic delta) near Unterstürmig, Franconian Jura.
3. Accumulation of snail shells, ¾ inch (2 cm), *Paraglauconia strombiformis* (Sowerby), from clay layers of the Lower Cretaceous period near Sachsenhagen.
4. *Dreissensia* (an Old World bivalve mollusk) quarry in the brackish-water deposits on the river Iller near Ulm (Kirchberg Formation).
5. A piece the size of a hand, 4¾ inches (12 cm), from the *Dreissensia* banks.

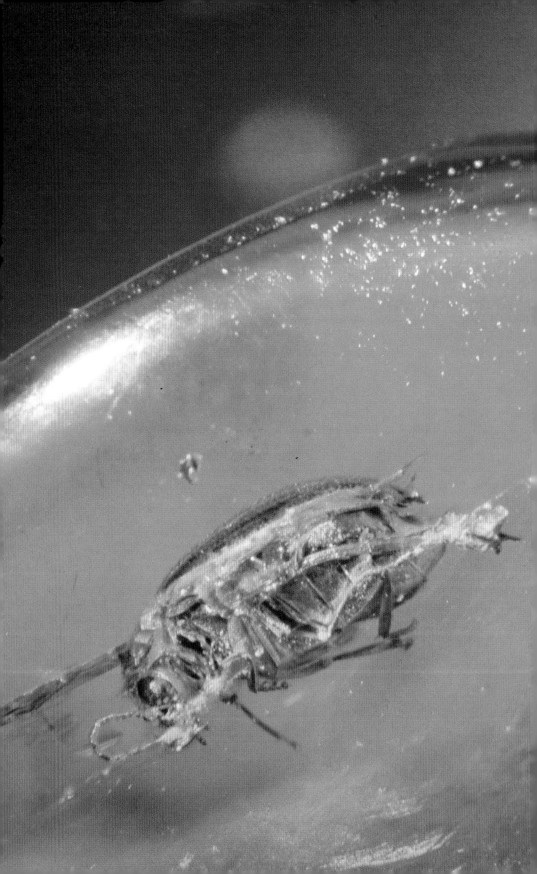

Life in Primeval Times

Fossil collectors should become familiar with the anatomy of plants and animals if they want to search for and prepare their remnants. In this book, I am only including a rough, incomplete outline of the development of the plant and animal world, intended as a suggestion for more intense study of the subject—for instance, by using professional literature.

Many specifics of the life of animals and plants in primeval times are still hidden or controversial, or not widely known. The drawings on the following pages are, therefore, only approximations of the shapes of ancient animals.

The Development of Life

Unbelievably slowly in the beginning, but then with an almost explosive tempo, plants and animals spread throughout the waters onto the land of the earth. Plants, of course, preceded animals, providing nutrition and environment for survival.

Life began in the oceans. Algae (in the form of algae limestone) began to accumulate in prehistoric times, often tinted black by coallike substances and bitumen-containing, shalelike deposits. Definitive fossil remnants appeared in the Cambrian period. During the Ordovician period, we begin to see the ap-

pearance of many types of invertebrates in extraordinary numbers. The first sprouting or budding plants appeared in shallow waters. Starting in the Silurian period, they moved onto dry land.

We see the first signs of organisms developing four limbs (Illus. 16, pg. 104). Beginning with the Devonian period, crustaceans, snails, scorpions, and four-limbed animals ventured out onto dry land, following the plant migration. Insects of today had their origins in the form of worms and crustaceans.

The first amphibians stayed in the marshlands near the coasts during the Devonian

Table 6. History of the Earth in Billions (10⁹) of Years △

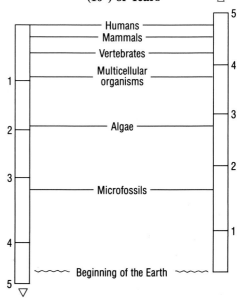

Plate 38

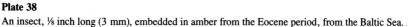
An insect, ⅛ inch long (3 mm), embedded in amber from the Eocene period, from the Baltic Sea.

Illus. 2. *Seymouria*. 24 inches long (60 cm), from the Permian period, is a link between amphibians and reptiles. Long considered to be the original reptile, according to new information, it is thought to belong to the reptiles of the Carboniferous period.

period, living in the water as well as on land. During the Carboniferous period, under subtropical conditions and in humid inland regions, the development of large club moss, horsetails and fern plants, the basic materials of hard coal, began.

Plants producing naked seeds and needle-bearing trees appeared in the Permian period and expanded further onto dry land. Reptiles, developing from the amphibians, were better able to protect themselves against dryness than amphibians were, and followed the landward movement of the plants.

The earth's "Middle Ages" (Mesozoic era) saw the appearance of new groups of animals, such as the true ammonites, higher sea-urchins, crustaceans, new groups of bivalves and snails, and bony fish. Under favorable living conditions, we see the first signs of giant reptiles developing. The forerunners of mammals and birdlike animals with teeth represented the bridges to mammals and birds. However, they did not reach maturity until the end of the Cretaceous period, when flowering plants producing coated seeds began to appear. Life on dry land exploded. Contrasting climates and also events that created the mountains changed land and oceans. New species began to appear. By the end of the Cretaceous period, ammonites, belemnites, and dinosaurs became extinct. It was the mammals, birds, snails, and higher orders of insects that profited most on the land; they populate the earth to this day.

The World of Plants (Flora)

Spores and Algae

In southern Africa, evidence of the following were discovered: spores, plantlike structures dating back 3 billion (3×10^9) years; organisms resembling bacteria, single-cell organisms dating back 2 billion years, which probably already had nuclei; and algaelike fossils. (It was also in southern Africa that what may be the earliest humanlike being was found: 2-million-year-old Olduvai man.) Single-cell microscopic, silicic algae, known as *diatoms*, were present from the Jurassic period on in such numbers that their skeletal remains could form silicious or diatomaceous earth.

Spore Plants

Multicellular organisms were first found in 700-million-year-old formations. Four hundred million years ago, during the change from the Silurian to the Devonian period naked seed ferns and leafless spore plant with vascular systems began to expand onto dry land. These primeval ferns were the forerunners of the higher spore plants that sprouted leaves from their buds. The giant lycopsid plants in the Carboniferous, like *Sigillaria* and *Lepidodendron*, left behind impressions of their bark (30–1, 30–2), as did many smaller, shrublike crawling or branching bushes.

Fern plants expanded throughout the Carboniferous period. The horsetail plants (sphenopsids) like *Equisetum* (7–1) appeared in the Devonian and were at their acme by the Carboniferous, when some like *Calamites*, reached tree height (30–3

Naked-Seed Plants (Gymnosperms)

During the time of the spore plants in the Carboniferous, naked-seed plants, or *gym*

** Illus. 3.** Plants from various ages of the earth. **1.** Psilophyte, Lower Devonian. **2.** *Sigillaria*, Carboniferous. **3.** *Lepidodendron*, Carboniferous. **4.** Horsetail plant, *Calamites*, Carboniferous. **5.** Cordaite, Carboniferous. **6.** Conifer, *Araucaria*, Permian. **7.** Ginkgo tree, Permian. **8.** Seed fern (pteridosperm), Carboniferous. **9.** Tree fern, Carboniferous.

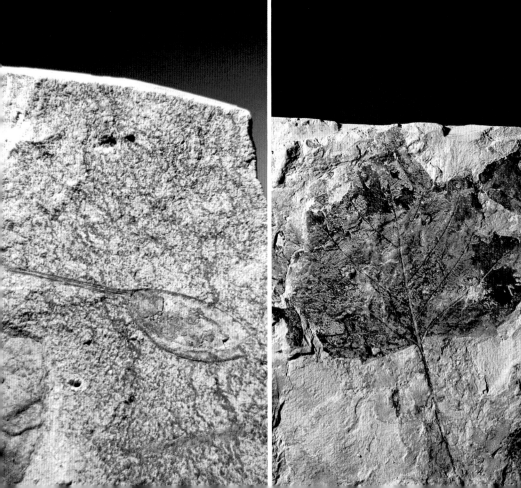

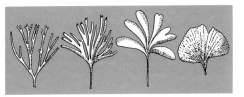

Illus. 4. The evolution of the ginkgo leaf from the Permian period (extreme left) to the Jurassic, the Cretaceous, and the present (extreme right).

nosperms, already existed. Their seeds were attached to the plant's seed-bearing leaves. Many have left fossil records. The conifer-like cordaite trees (named after the Prague botanist Corda) flourished during the Permian-Carboniferous. Some grew up to 130 feet (40 meters) tall. The ginkgoes were another group of gymnosperms. They were deciduous trees that appeared in the early Permian and became widespread in the Mesozoic. Their decline began in the Cretaceous. Today *Ginkgo biloba* is the only living ginkgo. Seed ferns (pteridosperms), another group of gymnosperms, appeared in the Upper Devonian and became abundant and diverse in the Carboniferous, but are now extinct. The cycadophytes, yet another group of gymnosperms, flourished during the Mesozoic and Cenozoic. One group, the cycadeoids, is extinct. Another group, the cycads, has some members that have survived to this day. (See Illus. 3 for examples.)

Covered-Seed Plants (Angiosperms)

Angiosperms, or flowering plants, are the dominant plants today. Their seeds are protected by an ovary. Pollen, which makes the existence of covered seeds possible, has been found in deposits from the Triassic and Jurassic periods. The angiosperms themselves are known since the Lower Cretaceous period and have dominated vegetation since the Tertiary period (see Plate 13). Almost all leaf-bearing trees, bushes, herbs, flowers, and grasses belong to the angiosperms (39-2, 39-3).

The World of Animals (Fauna)

No matter how difficult it might seem for the inexperienced fossil collector to determine that a mark in a rock deposit is an embedded fossil, he or she should take solace in the fact that in 1726 Johann Jakob Scheuchzer of Switzerland thought that the remains of a skeleton of a giant salamander from the Tertiary period were the remains of a man who had died during the Biblical flood.

Single-Celled Organisms

Some single-celled animal-like organisms leave skeletons, which are an important fossil record. Radiolaria, tiny one-celled marine animal-like creatures, have existed since the middle Cambrian. Their tiny skeletons are visible only under the microscope. Foraminifera, another group of one-celled marine organisms, can reach several centimeters in length. Foraminifera have existed since the Cambrian period. Nummulites, coin-shaped foraminifera of about 2⅜ inches (6 cm) in size, appeared in masses and contributed to Lower Tertiary nummulitic limestone (40-1).

Sponges (Porifera)

Tightly connected to the ground, the sponge has a hollow cavity and a porous outside wall. The skeleton is internal and may be organic

Plate 39

1. In a plate 6⅜ inches (16 cm) wide, a stem of horsetail *Neocalamites lehmannianus* Göppert, and leaf remnants, from the Rätolias near Kulmbach.

2. Ovary of *Podogonium*, 2¾ inches (7 cm), from the upper freshwater deposits of Heggbach near Biberach/Riss.

3. Leaf, 4 inches (10 cm), from a location comparable to the Öhningen plates from Schienerberg, near Radolfzell.

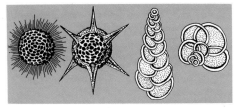

Illus. 5. Radiolaria, tiny, single-cell organisms with radiating siliceous skeletons (left and second from left), and foraminifera (right and second from right). These are two examples of single-celled organisms with chamberlike structures in their shells.

(a protein), or made of opaline silica, or of calcite and aragonite. Sponges live as individuals (40–3) or in colonies, where numerous generations of sponges build on the skeletons of previous ones. In this fashion, sponge colonies create reefs and sponge rocks.

Hydrozoa

Hydrozoa are a class of the phylum Cnidaria (previously called Coelenterata), a phylum that includes corals and jellyfish. The hydrozoan's life history alternates between a polyp phase and a free-swimming (medusa) jellyfish phase. Some hydrozoa have chitinous or calcareous skeletons.

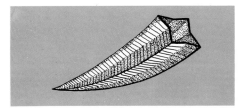

Illus. 6. Conularia, an extinct group probably related to jellyfish, lived as single individuals and were up to 2 inches (5 cm) long.

Conularia

Conularia are an extinct group that lived during the Paleozoic Era. They are thought to be related to Scyphozoa (jellyfish). Conularia left 4-sided cone-shaped chitinous *tests*, or coverings.

Corals

Corals have existed since the Ordovician period. They live as individuals as well as in reef-building colonies. Folded septa that divide the hollow coral bodies are typical (40–2), as is the aragonitic support skeleton. The coral animals live only in the upper portion of the skeleton.

Worms

Only a few early worms had hard body parts, and even those left only their boring tunnels behind. The fossils of tube worms with their chalklike shells were often attached to other fossil remnants (7–2 and 40–4).

Arthropods

Arthropods usually have a very thin, horny chitinous outer skin and pairs of jointed extremities. Spiders, scorpions, millipedes, insects, and crustaceans belong to this, the most versatile group of animals.

As far as fossils are concerned, only trilobites and crustaceans are important among the arthropods, because their chitinous exoskeletons often contain calcareous deposits, making them very resistant to damage. Insects, spiderlike animals, and millipedes are only fossilized under certain circumstances: for instance, in clay rock from the Carboniferous period; in limestone plates (26–2,

Plate 40

1. Nummulite limestone, 4 inches (10 cm) wide, from the Helvetian deposit, Eocene, near Neubeuren/Upper Bavaria.

2. Piece of coral from Nattheim near Heidenheim, with the typically radiating septa of the coral *Montlivaltia* (below) and *Trochoziatus* (above); Jurassic, Kimmeridgian (Malm epsilon); diameter of the corals; up to ¾ inch (2 cm).

3. Silica sponge *Siphonia*, 4 inches (10 cm), from the Upper Cretaceous near Paulmy, France.

4. A tube worm (*Serpula*) found the shell of an ammonite, ¾ inch (2 cm), *Echioceras*, as a resting place and adapted itself to the spiral shape of the "house" of its host (Jurassic, Sinemurian, Liassic beta).

26–3); embedded in amber (38); in later, Tertiary formations, like limestone plates from the Oligocene near Céreste (42) or the dysodile plates from the Maars in Randeck (65–3).

Trilobites

The skeleton of a trilobite is divided into the head plate (cephalon), the rump (thorax) with its segments, and the tail plate (pygidium). Two vertical grooves in the center of the back form a spindle shape. The two side parts of the thorax are called the pleurae. The middle part of the head is called the glabella. The parts on the side of the head are the cheeks. Many trilobites had eyes, but some were blind. For layers from the Cambrian on up to the Permian period, trilobites (10, 41, 43–1, 43–2) are used by fossil collectors and geologists as guide fossils.

Crustaceans

Crustaceans are a mostly aquatic class of arthropods, although some live on land. They are gill-breathing, have segmented bodies, and two pairs of antennae. Crustaceans include the branchiopods (water fleas); barnacles; decapods such as crabs and prawns; and ostracods, tiny aquatic crustaceans.

Branchiopods (water fleas) are tiny, primitive crustaceans with a one or two-valved carapace. They have been present from the Lower Devonian on. Ostracods, varying from 0.5 mm to 3/16 inch (5 mm) in size, first appeared in the Cambrian. Their bodies are enclosed in a two-valved carapace with chitinous outgrowths. They have 5–7 pairs of limbs.

Barnacles (subclass Cirripeda) such as *Balanus* (43–4) are stationary crustaceans

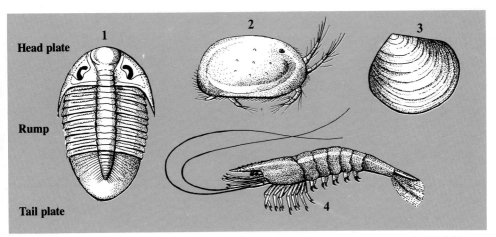

Illus. 7. Fossil arthropods. **1.** Trilobite *Dalmania*, 2 inches (5 cm) long, from the Silurian period. Trilobites have left numerous fossil records. **2.** An ostracod, a tiny aquatic crustacean only ⅛ inch (3 mm) in size, present since the Cambrian period. **3.** Branchiopods (water fleas) are also crustaceans; they have been found as early as Devonian times. **4.** A decapod, *Penaeus*, about 6 inches long (15 cm), present since the Permian period.

Plate 41
This trilobite, *Modocia typicalis* Martum, 1½ inches (4 cm) long, from the Cambrian Wheeler Formation, House Range, Millard County, Utah, was very well prepared.

that secrete calcareous plates. They have been present since the Upper Silurian. Decapods such as shrimp and crabs have front legs that are modified into pincers and a hard outer skeleton that includes a cephalothorax and abdomen. They have a single pair of legs for each body segment.

With a little bit of luck, the fossil collector might be able to find a well-preserved decapod such as *Pemphix sueuri* (43–3), embedded in hard limestone in ceratitic deposits of the Triassic period. Compressed decapods can also be found in clay deposits as well as in limestone plates, and enclosed in concretions (33).

Brachiopods

Brachiopods are a phylum of sessile marine animals that secrete calcareous or chitinous shells. Brachiopods (44–1) usually have smaller upper and larger lower shells. The shell has a hole to accommodate a horny pedicle, which is used for anchorage. Brachiopods reached their largest diversity during the Paleozoic era; 140 species of brachiopods have survived. The collector often can find brachiopods in layers of weathered rocks (21–1). Most brachiopods range in size from ⅞ inch to 3 inches (2 to 7 cm), although some are much larger or smaller.

Sea Mosses (Bryozoa)

Bryozoa are a phylum of small colonial, sessile marine animals, whose soft body parts are very similar to those of the brachiopods. Although individual animals are only 1 mm in size, they form massive colonies or stem-like structures and were important in reef formation. Bryozoan colonies have been found in all formations from the Ordovician period onwards. In formations from the later Tertiary period, the fossil collector will find them in limestone remnants, in the shape of strawberries (11–2) or as delicately perforated, round structures (44–2). Remnants of bryozoan colonies from the Carboniferous period, notable for their screw-shaped central axes, can be found near Floraville, Illinois (25–2).

Bivalve Mollusks

Bivalve mollusks have two-sided shells (or valves), like the brachiopods do. However, the shells are positioned to the left and right side of the soft body. Shells are composed of either calcite or aragonite, which tends to make fossilization easy. Identifying characteristics, in addition to the shape of the shell, are the muscular attachments of the shell's locking and closing mechanism (44–3, 44–4). Clams, scallops, oysters, and mussels are some familiar bivalves.

Gastropods

The gastropods, of which there exist approximately 30,000 varieties, are the most numerous class of mollusks. They are both aquatic and terrestrial. The gastropod's calcite or aragonite shell is a single (univalve) structure that is usually spiral shaped, but

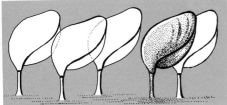
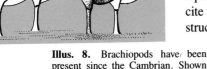

Illus. 8. Brachiopods have been present since the Cambrian. Shown here, well-known terebratulids from the Devonian period.

Plate 42
For 30 million years this fly, ⅝ inch (1.5 cm) in size, rested on a limestone plate of the Oligocene period near Céreste, Provence, France.

occasionally it can also be bowl-shaped (45–5). The shape and ornamentation of the shell are important for identification purposes, as is the configuration of the aperture. A *steinkern* seldom is a good guide for identifying a specimen. Snails, slugs, and whelks are some examples of gastropods. Gastropods have existed from the Cambrian to recent times.

The preparation of some gastropod *steinkerns* from the iron-rich Jurassic deposits of the Dogger gamma (Bajocian stage, see 45–1 to 45–4) might serve as good example of the difficulty in identifying a snail and how easily it can be mistaken for an ammonite. Gastropods increased vastly in numbers and diversity by the Tertiary period (12–1, 12–2).

Cephalopods

Head and foot are closely associated in the organisms called cephalopods, which belong

Illus. 9. *Nautilus*, a living fossil.

to the phylum Mollusca (mollusks). Some species of this group are cuttlefish, nautiloids, ammonites, and belemnites. The latter two have been extinct since the end of the Cretaceous period. The cephalopod's shell is a chambered shell that is connected by a continuous tunnel (siphuncle). In belem-

Plate 43 (page 90)
1. Trilobite *Phacops*, 2⅜ inches (6 cm), from deposits from the Devonian period in France. The head plate with glabella and the thoracic plate, including the segments (pleura), are visible. The tail plate (pygidium) is bent under the thorax.
2. Trilobite *Elrathia kingii* (Meek), ¾ inch (2 cm), with the typical three-part vertical and horizontal division, from the Middle Cambrian period, belonging to the family of Olenoides, from Utah.
3. Decapod *Pemphix sueuri* Desmarest, 3⅛ inches (8 cm), from the Triassic period, upper shell limestone, near Haigerloch, Swabian Alps.
4. A group of *Balanus* barnacles, ⅜-inch-long (1 cm) each, grown onto a terebratulid; Oligocene, from Astrup near Osnabrück.

Plate 44 (page 92)
1. *Terebratula grandis*, 2⅜ inches (6 cm), from deposits of the Oligocene period at Astrup near Osnabrück; the left sample shows *Balanus* attached to the edge of the shell.
2. Calcified colonies, 1½ inches long (4 cm), of a bryozoan, *Ceriopora simplex* Miller, showing the hole made by a mollusk, from the sand of the upper sea deposits near Ursendorf.
3. *Axinea obovata* (Lamarck), a 3-inch (8-cm) bivalve mollusk from the Oligocene, clearly showing valve, ligament, impression of the sphincter-muscle attachment, and markings at the edge of the shell.
4. Oyster *Liostrea eduliformis* (Schlotheim), 4¾ inches (12 cm) long, from the Jurassic Bajocian stage (Dogger delta) near Gosheim, Swabian Alps. The shell has been brush-cleaned; it is asymmetrical and platelike, similar to that of today's oyster.

Plate 45 (page 93)
1–4. The *steinkern* from the snail *Pleurotomaria*, 3⅛ inches (8 cm), from the Dogger gamma level near Nenningen. The only way to differentiate it from an ammonite was the elevated first coil. A growth containing oysters was discovered during preparation.
5. *Actaeonella*, a sea snail from the Gosau Cretaceous in Brandenberg, Tyrol; left, a cross-section; right, a vertical section.

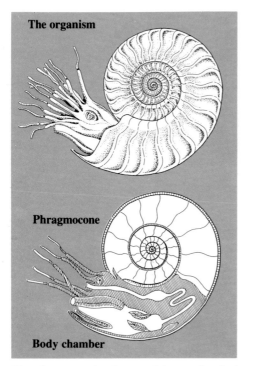

The organism

Phragmocone

Body chamber

Illus. 10. Ammonite, diagram of the organism (*top*) and cross-section (*bottom*).

nites, ammonites, and nautiloids, the inner chambers of the shell are believed to have been air-filled. This part is called the phragmocone. The soft-bodied animal lived in the outermost chamber of the shell (body chamber).

Nautiloids
Nautiloids, the earliest cephalopods, appeared in the late Cambrian. Early nautiloids were small and had slightly curved shells and close-set septa (the walls dividing the shell). In the Ordovician they diversified and had a variety of shell shapes, including straight (orthocones) and coiled shapes. The chambered phragmocone contains a gas in *Nautilus*, the only living member of the species, which increases the animal's buoyancy. Nautiloids nearly became extinct at the end of the Triassic period.

Ammonoids
Ammonoids were cephalopods that lived from the Devonian to the end of the Cretaceous period. They had coiled, planispiral shells made of aragonite. Some reached 100 inches (250 cm) in diameter. The shell consisted of three parts, the embryonic shell (protoconch), the phragmocone, and the body chamber (see Illus. 10). There were a variety of ammonite shapes and sizes. The suture lines, where the septa of the chamber met the shell wall, were often complex; they are an aid to identifying the various ammonoids, which are classified in subgroups by the shapes of their suture lines as goniatitids (50–5), ceratitids (22–2, 22–3), prolecanitids, and clymeniids. The original ammonoids had many radiations, interrupted by many extinctions: goniatitids and clymeniids (later Devonian); new families of goniatitids in the Carboniferous–Permian; ceratitids (Triassic); and ammonitids (Jurassic–Cretaceous). During the Lower Carboniferous, an offshoot of the ceratitids, the prolecanitids, arose. Both ammonoids and

Plate 46 (page 95)
Discoscaphites conradi, 2⅜ inches (6 cm) long, is one of the most beautiful ammonites; it is slightly coiled and has an opalized shell; from the Fox Hills Formation of the Upper Cretaceous in South Dakota.

Plate 47 (page 96)
1. *Pachydiscus* sp., an ammonite 5½ inches (14 cm) long, was embedded in Cretaceous limestone deposits of the Fox Hills Formation, South Dakota. The white remnants of the shell were removed so that the lobe line of the *steinkern*, very important for identification, would be clearly visible.
2. *Placenticeras meeki*, a Cretaceous ammonite from the Fox Hills Formation of South Dakota, 6⅜ inches wide (16 cm). The *steinkern* shows very vivid suture lines.

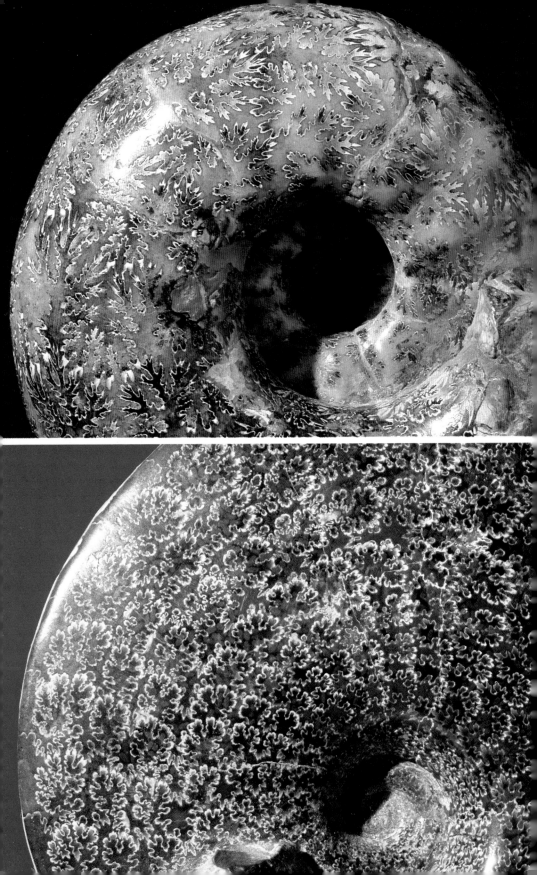

nautiloids have spiral-coiled shells. However, the walls of the chambers of the ammonoids are more sharply folded (50–2), which causes their lobelines to be much deeper. Damaged ammonites (50–4), and some that are sawn in half (59–1), show characteristic chambers, sometimes with crystals present in the phragmocone.

Cephalopods without an Outer Shell (Coleoids)

In coleoids, a subclass of cephalopods, the soft body grows around the phragmocone, making the phragmocone an inner shell. Belemnites, an extinct order of coleoids, are common fossils in the Jurassic and Cretaceous. The phragmocone of belemnites was short and was inside a cavity, the alveolus, which was protected by the guard, a solid, calcitic, cigar-shaped structure (48–1). To find a guard with all the parts of the phragmocone intact is very difficult. Exceptions are in belemnites in which the soft parts are preserved, like those found in the shale deposits of the Black Jurassic epsilon (Toarcian stage). Giant guards, more than 39 inches (1 meter) in length, are usually found broken into smaller pieces (48–3), with tube worms (32–3) or oysters attached. In the cuttlefish, which has tentacles like the belemnite, very little of the phragmocone is left. The *Spirula* (52–2), however, still has a

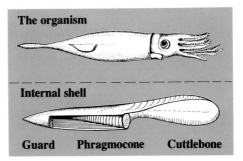

The organism

Internal shell

Guard   **Phragmocone**   **Cuttlebone**

Illus. 11. Belemnite, drawing of the organism and the internal shell.

chambered, coiled shell. What used to be the body chamber of the organism has changed to a flat plate. The cuttlebone carried by the Teuthida, or squid, is a modified phragmocone that is reduced to a horny "pen." In the octopus, the shell is missing altogether.

Echinoderms

Echinoderms are a phylum that includes sea lilies (Crinoidea), sea-urchins (Echnoidea), starfish (Asteroidea), brittle stars (Ophiuroidea), and sea cucumbers (Holothuroidea). They are distinguished from other species by their five-rayed symmetry and ambulacral grooves containing the water vascular system, used to breathe, eat, feel, and move about. The internal skeleton (test) of the echinoderm consists of a number of small plates, each of which is a single calcite crystal.

Plate 48 (page 98)

1. This exposed belemnite rostrum, totaling 4¾ inches (12 cm), from the Jurassic Aalenian stage (Dogger beta) in the Wuchtal region, shows the pointed tip of the chambered phragmocone.

2. Belemnite, 7⅛ inches (18 cm), from the Jurassic Upper Pliensbachian stage (Liassic delta) from Göppingen, with guard, showing the largest part of the phragmocone, with its few chambers still preserved.

3. The remaining parts of the belemnite *Megateuthis giganteus*, 18 inches (45 cm), still have to be glued together (see Plate 32).

Plate 49 (page 99)

1. Fossil cast of ammonite *Perisphinctes*, 6 inches (15 cm) wide, from the Jurassic Kimmeridgian stage (Malm gamma) near Geisingen/Danube.

2. Stone core of two *Acanthopleuroceras maugenesti* (D'Orbigny), 3⅛ and 5⅜ inches (8 and 13 cm), ammonites from marl deposits of the Jurassic Lower Pliensbachian stage (Liassic gamma), colored black from coal deposits.

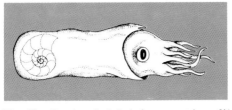

Illus. 12. Drawing of a *Spirula* from recent times, 3⅛ inches (8 cm) long. The chambered inner skeleton is drawn on the body.

Sea Lilies (Crinoids)

Most sea lilies are sedentary. The sea lily attaches itself to the ocean floor with rootlike structures (52–1). The sea lily carries its body in a bell-shaped crown, to which long arms are attached, on a stem that is usually long. Crinoids were particularly abundant during the Silurian period of the Paleozoic. Sea lily stems are often found in layered deposits or in rock formations (37–1). Small floating sea lilies are often found in limestone plates in Solnhofen (24–3). Related forms have been found in the rock-forming Alpine Triassic. Along with sea lilies, other echinoderms also inhabited the ocean floor during the Paleozoic, as discussed below.

Starfish (Asteroids) and Brittle Stars (Ophiuroids)

Starfish and brittle stars are usually vagrant. They have five arms. The molds of the traces of resting starfish in fine-grained sandstone (2–2, 66–3) are well known, as are the embedded remnants of delicate brittle stars

in limestone plates from Solnhofen (27–1). Collectors in the United States have found well-preserved starfish from the Tertiary-Paleocene period near Los Angeles, California, in hard, shimmery sandstone deposits (51). Starfish also have been found at sites from the middle Devonian period near Mt. Marion Beds, Hamilton.

Sea-Urchins (Echinoids)

Echinoids are the most versatile forms of all of the echinoderms. They are known to have existed since the Ordovician period. Sea-

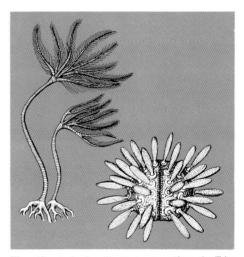

Illus. 13. *Left:* Sea lily *Pentacrinus* (from the Triassic), with rootlike feet. Stem and crown are typical of the sea lily from the Ordovician period on. *Right:* Sea-urchin *Cidaris* with spines (from the Jurassic) is typical of sea-urchins from the Ordovician period on.

Plate 50

1. *Nautilus* with body chamber, 4¾ inches (12 cm) long, from the Jurassic Lower Pliensbachian stage (Liassic gamma), from Tuningen, Swabian Alps.

2. Septum, 2⅜ inches (6 cm) wide, of an ammonite, *Aspidoceras*, from the Jurassic Tithonian stage (Malm zeta) from Laisacker near Neuburg/Danube; showing saddles, forward-curving structures domed in the direction of the mouth, and backward-bent folds called lobes.

3. This is an ammonite without a shell. The position of the septa and lobelines left an impression on the *steinkern*.

4. *Staufenia*, 4 inches (10 cm) wide, an ammonite that broke open during excavation, from the Jurassic Aalenian stage (Dogger beta) near Blumberg. It shows calcite crystals in chambers of the phragmocone and a partially filled body chamber.

5. Goniatite *Cheiloceras*, ¾ inch (18 mm) wide, from the Upper Devonian period in Nehden near Brilon.

6. One of the best-known ammonites from the Jurassic is the *Amaltheus margaritatus* Montfort, here 2 inches wide (5 cm), from the Upper Pliensbachian (Liassic delta) from Göppingen.

urchins have developed skeleton capsules (tests) that are either ball-, disk-, or heart-shaped. They have their mouths on the underside and their anal openings on top. Their calcite plates carry differently shaped spines. In the United States, sea-urchins have been found in Miocene sandstone in the Cuyana Valley, California (51–1) and in Tertiary-Miocene deposits from San Diego, California (51–3).

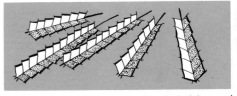

Illus. 14. Graptolites from the Ordovician and Silurian.

Sea Cucumbers (Holothuroids)
Sea cucumbers are small, sausage-shaped bottom dwellers that first appeared in the Ordovician period. There are about 500 known living species. They do not have arms or spines, but small calcareous ossicles.

Graptolites
Graptolites consist of chitinous masses of extinct colonial marine organisms, whose branchlike structures existed from the Ordivician to the Devonian periods. They are generally included in the phylum Hemicordata. During the Ordovician and Silurian periods, they formed the basis of graptolite shale. Some forms were colonies that were sessile and tightly grown together; some groups probably floated on the water.

Vertebrates
Vertebrates, with their typically jointed spinal column, are the largest and most diverse group of chordates. For the fossil collector, the primeval fish is the most sought after, as well as the most obtainable fossil.

Of course, the collector can also discover the remnants of amphibians, reptiles, birds, and mammals. These finds can be of enormous value for scientific research. However, excavating whole skeletons goes beyond the expertise of an amateur fossil collector. It is best to leave such projects to the scientifically trained expert.

Fish
Fish are the most primitive of all vertebrates. Jawless fish (Agnatha) are at the beginning of the developmental stages of fish. They are represented today by the lamprey and the hagfish. Extinct forms of fish, ostracoderms, were mostly heavily armored and had cartilage endoskeletons; they were bottom-living. Agnatha became extinct at the end of the Devonian.

Placoderms, now extinct, were the first fish with jaws, which had primitive, toothlike bony plates in them. Their bodies resembled those of today's sharks. They had a partly bony, cartilaginous inner skeleton and some had a scaly skin cover. The tail fin was asymmetric. Placoderms were already diversified when they appeared in the Upper Silurian. Few survived into the early Carboniferous.

Chondrichthyes, which include sharks and rays, have an endoskeleton of cartilage and open gill slits. Fossils of Chondrichthyes appeared as early as the Devonian period. Bony tissue is missing and the skin is covered with tiny, toothlike scales or denticles.

Plate 51
1. Sea urchin *Astrodapsis arnoldi*, 2 inches (5 cm) long, was found in Miocene sandstone in the Cuyana Valley, California.
2. *Ventura henrica*, 1.4 inches (3.5 cm) long, from the Tertiary-Paleocene period, near Los Angeles. Several starfish are intact—a rare find.
3. Sea urchin *Dendraster venturaensis*, 3.2 inches (8 cm) long, from the Tertiary-Miocene period, from San Diego, California.

During the Devonian, bony fish (Osteichthyes) arose. By the lower Devonian, they were already defined into two groups: ray-finned Actinopterygii and fleshy finned Sarcopterygii. Dipnoi (lungfish) and Crossopterygii (fringe or tassel-finned fishes) were two groups of Sarcopterygii. Early ray-finned fish, chondrosteans, were strong-swimming predators, whose bodies were covered by thick, shiny enamel-covered bony scales of rhombic shape (ganoid scales) (54–1, 54–2, 54–3). By the Cretaceous, another subclass of Actinopterygii, Teleosti (higher fishes), became dominant. Bony fish today outnumber other types of fish. They usually have thin scales, a swim bladder (a gas-filled organ that helps maintain buoyancy), a symmetrical, shortened tail, and gill covers over the gill chambers (25, 54–4).

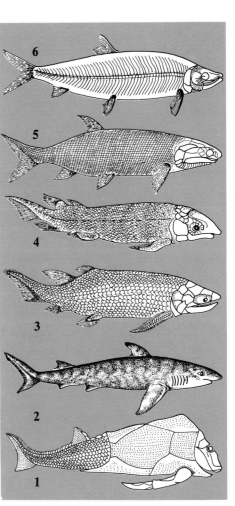

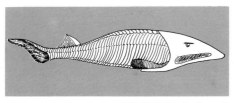

Illus. 15 (above). Jawless fish *Cephalaspis*, from the Silurian/Devonian period.

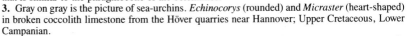

Illus. 16 (right). The group of jawed fish includes armored fish (placoderms), cartilaginous fish (Chondrichthyes), and bony fish (Osteichthyes). **1.** Placoderm *Pterichthyodes* with two armlike fins; Devonian. **2.** One of the first Chondrichthyes, *Cladoselache*, Devonian, a forerunner of today's sharks. Their teeth, when worn off, fall out and are replaced by new teeth. Teeth in the upper jaw are usually wide with jagged edges; teeth in the lower jaw are smaller with smooth edges. **3.** Crossoptyerygii (tassel-finned fish) from the Devonian. **4.** *Dipnoi* (lungfish) from the Devonian. **5.** *Actinopterygii* (ray-finned fish) with ganoid scales, Devonian. **6.** Modern bony fish (Teleosti) from the Jurassic period.

Plate 52

1. Two sea lilies (*Millericrinus*) from the Jurassic Oxfordian stage (Malm alpha), from Liesberg near Basel, with strong rootlike feet visible on the large fracture plane; 2 inches (5 cm) long. The violet tint is typical for this specimen.
2. Coiled inner shell, ¾ inch (2 cm), of a recent cuttlefish, *Spirula*, with a smooth chamber septum that is similar to the phragmocone of the belemnites.
3. Gray on gray is the picture of sea-urchins. *Echinocorys* (rounded) and *Micraster* (heart-shaped) in broken coccolith limestone from the Höver quarries near Hannover; Upper Cretaceous, Lower Campanian.
4. *Diplopodia subangularis* (Goldfuss), ⅜ inches (1 cm), an ordinary sea-urchin from the Jurassic Oxfordian stage (Malm alpha) near Blumberg.
5. From the Upper Cretaceous Turonian stage near Wüllen come the small, ½-inch (1.5 cm) sea-urchins, *Conulus* (*left*) and *Micraster* (*right*). The large sea-urchin (4 inches or 10 cm), *Hemipneustes* (*middle*), was found near Maastricht.

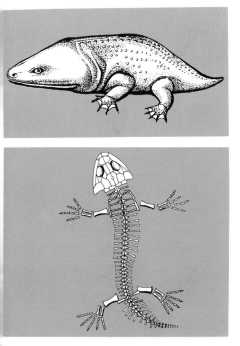

Illus. 17 (top). *Metoposaurus*, up to 4 feet long (120 cm), an amphibian from the Triassic period.

Illus. 18 (bottom). Skeleton of *Branchiosaurus*, 2 inches long (5 cm), an amphibian from the Permian period.

Illus. 19 (top). *Placodus*, up to 5 feet (150 cm) in size, a reptile from the Triassic period.

Illus. 20 (bottom). Primeval bird, *Archaeopteryx*, approximately the size of a pigeon, Jurassic period.

Amphibians

In the Devonian, the crossopterygians already had nasal-throat passages and an air bladder that functioned as an additional breathing organ (lung). Crossopterygians are considered the ancestors of the amphibians and the land vertebrates. The *Stegocephalia*, the forerunner of the salamander, existed in the Devonian, living alternately in the water and on the land. The widely distributed, small *Branchiosaurus* (55–1) of the Permian period is another early amphibian.

Reptiles

Reptiles breathe with lungs and lay shell-covered eggs that lie in a fluid-filled sac (amnion). Because their skin is covered with scales, reptiles can live away from the water, on land. Reptiles developed from the primeval types of the Carboniferous period. Under very favorable environmental conditions, dinosaurs evolved, starting in the late Triassic. Some grew to giant size. Marine reptiles like ichthyosaurs lived in the ocean; dinosaurs lived on land, and flying reptiles such as

Plate 53
The sea lily *Japocrinus colletti*, 1½ inches (4 cm), dating from the Carboniferous-Mississippian, from Crawfordsville, Indiana.

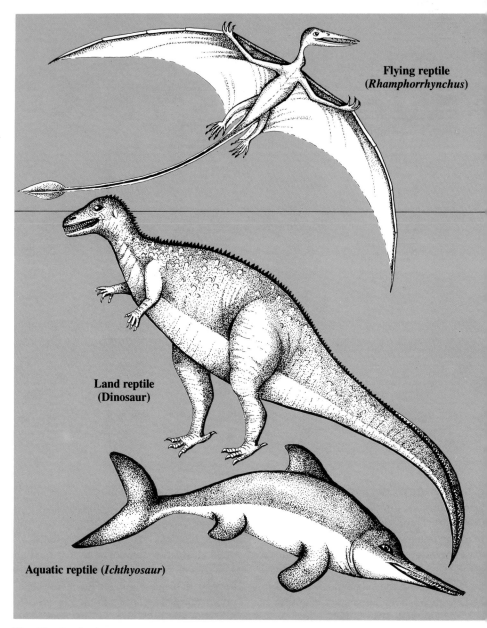

Flying reptile
(*Rhamphorrhynchus*)

Land reptile
(Dinosaur)

Aquatic reptile (*Ichthyosaur*)

Illus. 21. Reptiles from the Jurassic and Cretaceous periods. *Top*, a flying reptile, *Rhamphorrhynchus*; *middle*, a dinosaur; *bottom*, an ichthyosaur, a marine reptile.

Plate 54

1	2
3	
4	

1. The front of a compressed scaly fish, 5½ inches long (14 cm), from the Lower Permian period, from Heimerkirchen. The head is only partially excavated.

2. The back portion of an *Amplypterus*, 4 inches long (10 cm), from the same layer as 1, but from Cölln/Pfalz. Heavy weathering has changed the original fossil color.

3. Crocodile fish *Lepisosteus strausi*, 10 inches long (25 cm), from the Eocene, from Messel, with an imposing coat of scales, seen after costly preparation with synthetic resin.

4. *Leptolepis sprattiformis*, 3⅛ inches long (8 cm), a typical fossil found in limestone plate deposits from the Altmühl Valley; Jurassic, Tithonian stage (Malm zeta).

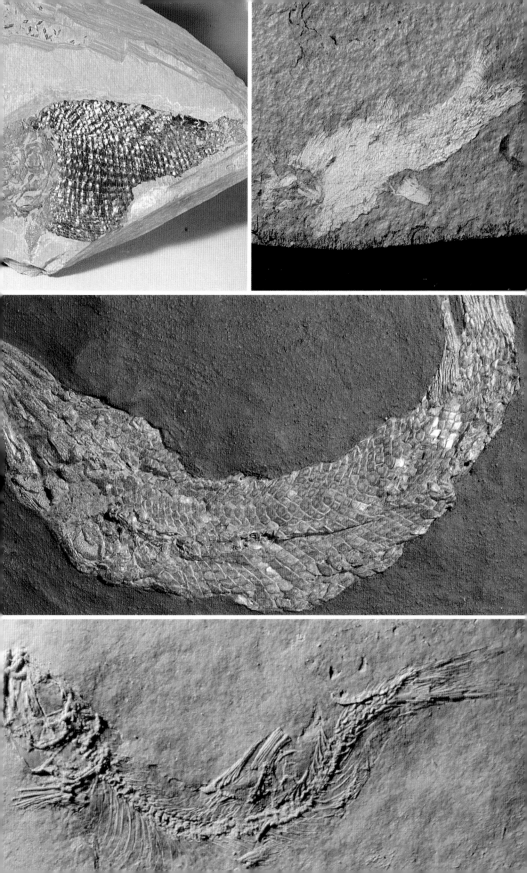

Rhamphorrhynchus could fly through the air. With the end of the Cretaceous period, the early reptiles became extinct.

Finding reptile traces (2–1), vertebra from a marine reptile (32–5), or perhaps teeth from a *Placodus* (55–2) delights and astounds the fossil collector. There are many locations in the United States where dinosaur fossils have been found. Among the oldest reptiles found are those from the Carboniferous Pennsylvanian period in Linton, Ohio; the marine reptile *Mosasaurus* from the Cretaceous Niobrara Chalk in Kansas; the dinosaur skeletons of *Brontosaurus* and *Stegosaurus* from the Upper Jurassic Morrison Formation in Como Bluff, Wyoming; *Tyrannosaurus*, a carnivorous dinosaur from the Upper Cretaceous period in the Hell Creek Basin, Montana; and a duck-billed dinosaur from the Upper Cretaceous period in Converse County, Wyoming. Dinosaur traces in sandstone from the Triassic period in the United States have been found, among other places, in Turner Falls, Massachusetts (with indentations from raindrops) and in Paluxy Creek, Texas.

Birds (Aves)

It is astounding that warm-blooded birds evolved from reptiles that were very similar to dinosaurs. In the limestone blocks in Solnhofen, we discovered time and again remains of the primeval bird *Archaeopteryx*. The presence of bird fossils, particularly in sediments from the Tertiary period, are well-known. They are relatively rare, because the environment in which they lived was not conducive to the formation of fossils.

Mammals

Small, primitive mammals, 8 to 12 inches (20 to 30 cm) long, are well-known from the end of the Triassic to the Jurassic period. However, it wasn't until the transitional period of the Cretaceous to the Tertiary that warm-blooded mammals, equipped with special chewing mechanisms, appeared. A diversity, still not well understood, gave rise to today's mammals. Teeth, the most robust part of mammals, are what the fossil collector will probably find. They make definite identification possible, because they are all shaped differently, depending on the animal's diet. Mammals owe their rapid and diverse development, in addition to their special set of teeth, to the fact that they give birth to live young.

Finds from the later Tertiary period, like those from the deposits of the Eocene in the Geisel Valley near Halle or in the oil shale plates from Messel, are of immense importance; they give us new information about the history of the evolution of the mammals.

Guide Fossils

Guide fossils are the fossilized remnants of plants and animals that lived over a wide region for a relatively short time span, in sufficient numbers to be present in distinct deposits and locations; they therefore are useful for organizing a timetable of the history of the earth.

Trilobites (Cambrian), graptolites (Ordovician to Silurian), and ammonites (Devonian to Cretaceous) are typical guide fossils for their respective historical periods. However, other fossils from animal and plant remnants serve as guide fossils as well.

Plate 55

1. Remains of a skeleton of a *Branchiosaurus*, 2 inches (5 cm), an amphibian from the Lower Permian period.
2. Portion of a cast of a front tooth, 1½ inches (3.5 cm) long, from a *Placodus*, a reptile from the Middle Triassic period, near Haigerloch.

Tools and Methods of Preparation

For his or her first outing, the fossil collector will probably use the tools he or she already has on hand. It is not until later, in the company of fellow collectors, that the new collector realizes that there are more practical tools available. In addition, actually working in the field and gaining experience is a good teacher. In time, while shopping in a hardware store, for instance, the collector will come across tools that are seemingly ideal for fossil preparation, even though they might have been intended for something entirely different. The best example I can cite is the asparagus cutter, which I find ideal for working in soft deposits or sediments. Special mail-order houses dealing exclusively with items relating to minerals and fossils offer equipment and tools needed to work with rocks in the field and to prepare fossils at home. For every craftsman, and every fossil collector, proper tools are the key to success; they also save time and increase enjoyment in the work. Suggestions as to what constitutes a proper tool are intended to avoid unnecessary detours, but they do not take the place of the collector's own experience. A visit with a stonemason will provide additional valuable information as to the choice of the right tools.

Those collectors who work as scientists or specialists are particularly interested in preserving minute fossil details and in the conditions under which the fossils were em-

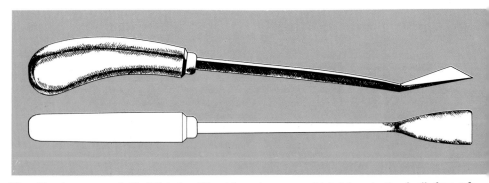

Illus. 22. An asparagus knife, 17½ inches (44 cm) long, is a very useful tool for extracting fossils from soft material.

Illus. 23. Tools for excavating fossil

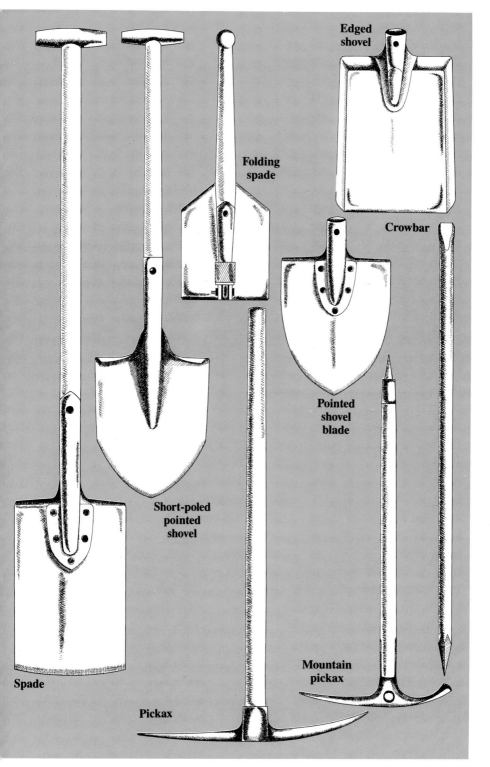

Folding
spade

Edged
shovel

Crowbar

Pointed
shovel
blade

Short-poled
pointed
shovel

Spade

Pickax

Mountain
pickax

113

bedded. The amateur fossil collector has different priorities. When the amateur comes across shells or remains of ammonite fossils, for instance, he or she is interested in displaying the find at home. For the amateur, the visible effect—the beauty of the object—is what counts. Even while still extracting a fossil, he or she may want to think about what to do with the find—for instance, whether or not it is necessary to remove all the deposits surrounding the fossil.

I often like to free only part of the fossil, so that it remains part of the rock in which it is embedded. Such partial preparation of a fossil remnant, creating what amounts to a relief (49), is often more work than removing all the surrounding rock deposits, because one not only has to pay attention to the fossil itself, but also to the rock surrounding it. Not many finds lend themselves to this type of display. Nevertheless, it always is important to make sure that a sufficiently large rock is excavated and taken home. There, in peace and quiet, the collector can do a thorough cleaning job and decide on which way to proceed.

Extracting Fossil-Containing Deposits

Much preliminary work has to be done before one can begin to dig for fossils in fossil-containing deposits. Weathered debris needs to be removed in order to reach the layers where fossils might be embedded. A shovel, pickax, and crowbar are absolute necessities (see Illus. 23).

A long-shafted shovel with a blade that is pointed at the lower edge is particularly suited for clearing loose rock debris and rough gravel. A standard-length shaft eliminates much of the bending down, making the job easier. Despite this advantage, I often prefer a shovel with a shorter pole and a handle on the end, one with the blade rolled up on the upper edge (see Illus. 23). Such a

shovel is easily stored in the trunk of a car, easy to carry while walking, and very handy when working in narrow, small places. It is also easy to push your foot on the rounded edge when you dig.

A shovel with an angled edge is very useful for moving soft, sandy, fine-grained material. This shovel is also very good for handling thick, viscous material.

The spade is used to dig ditches or deep holes. A fold-up spade is a great favorite, since it is easy to transport.

Pickaxes are used to loosen hard ground or rock formations, but they are also very effective for freeing large rocks. They are approximately 16 inches (40 cm) long and differ in weight. A lighter pickax is good for loosening soft ground; a heavier one is better for loosening rocks. The pointed end is used for loosening material; the blunt end, for scraping.

For many fossil collectors, the mountaineer's pickax is the ideal tool. It serves as a support when maneuvering in narrow, steep, and rough terrain. At the desired location, it is perfect for extracting rock samples. It is also a good tool for scraping.

The crowbar is helpful when a hammer and a pickax are not sufficient to do the job. It is almost 39 inches (1 m) long, with a blunt end and a pointed end. Its leverage can be used effectively to move rocks.

Preparation with Hammer and Chisel

Some Useful Hammers

Hammers and chisels, available in different sizes, are the tools most often used for preparing fossils. Because freeing fossils takes experience and knowledge, care and patience are the order of the day for the beginner.

Illus. 24.   Different types of useful hammers.

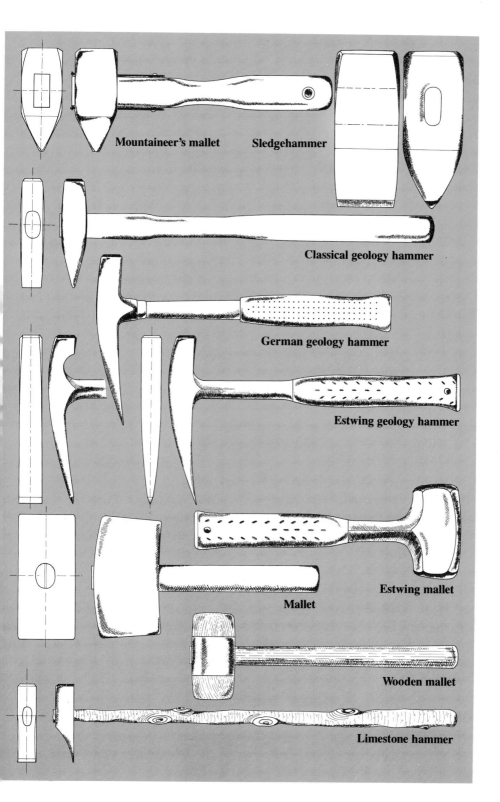

Mountaineer's mallet Sledgehammer

Classical geology hammer

German geology hammer

Estwing geology hammer

Estwing mallet

Mallet

Wooden mallet

Limestone hammer

Among the many different types of hammers, those made from hardened, quality tool steel are most suitable for working in rock quarries. The shaft is usually made from either maple or ash wood and is secured in the head with a metal splint. The length of the shaft determines the amount of the centrifugal force you have, and therefore, the technique used with the hammer. When the weight of the hammer is in a favorable relation to the length of the shaft, the user can save energy. Wooden shafts will dry out over time. If the head of the hammer becomes loose, immerse it and the shaft in water. The wood will expand, and the head will again be secure in the shaft. Hammer heads secured with plastic or metal splints do not come loose. A hammer should be held at the end of the shaft so that the centrifugal force of the head can be used efficiently (56–1).

A sledgehammer is useful for separating, removing, or shattering rocks. The weight of this hammer should be chosen according to the user's strength. The shaft is approximately 30 inches (75 cm) long. The head is flat on one side and pointed on the other. Since heavy tools can cause considerable damage, their use is restricted, particularly if the location of the fossil search is on private property. At other locations, such as landfills or on banks created during road construction, using a sledgehammer is a distinct advantage where a fossil can be freed with one rough swing of the hammer.

In general, smaller versions of the sledgehammer are sufficient for the needs of a fossil collector. They either have a short shaft or are made out of one piece of steel, weighing anywhere from 2 to 4 pounds (1 to 1.5 kg). Some sledgehammers are flat on both ends. They are useful for breaking up larger pieces of rock. Because of the flat ends, they also are ideal when working with a chisel.

A lighter version, used by mountain climbers, called the mountaineer's mallet, is useful for cutting pieces of rock to size, to open up rock nodules that are held in the palm of the hand (56–2), and for initial, rough preparation with hammer and chisel at the location or at home. The hand fits well around the specially shaped shaft. The head, with one flat side and a chisellike edge on the other side, is secured at the wooden shaft by a special steel band. Weighing only 1 pound (500 g), this hammer is ideal for young people out on an excursion.

The classical geology hammer weighs anywhere from 5 to 20 ounces (150 to 600 g). The head is made from special steel and is attached to a shaft about 16 inches (40 cm) long. One end of the head is flat; the other is shaped into a cutting edge. The hammer that weighs 5 ounces (150 g) is my favorite, because it is as efficient for careful work on location as it is for work with small chisels at home.

The German geology hammer is known for its excellent balance. When dealing with hard deposits, I use the one that is flat and square on one end and pointed on the other. For softer deposits, there is a head that is also flat and square, but whose other end is shaped for scraping.

The German geology hammer has a steel-tube handle and the shaft is cushioned with a soft, springy foam cover to absorb the impact when it strikes rocks. All geological hammers that are made from hard tool steel (and most of them are) should never be used as chisels. The steel may chip and splinter, causing severe injuries. This danger can be avoided, or at least reduced, by using a wood hammer instead, where no chipping can occur. The danger also can be diminished when the blows striking a piece of rock are gentle and careful and the tool is in impeccable condition. Goggles or safety glasses should be worn to protect the eyes when any cutting or chipping is done.

The Estwing geological hammer is made

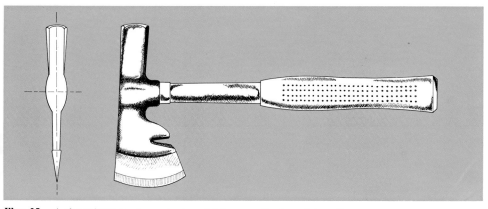

Illus. 25. A plaster hatchet, whose edge is useful for separating layered deposits.

of one piece of a special steel. The shaft is covered with a springy, resistant, nylon covering. There are two different types: a pickax and a scraping tool. Estwing hammers also come in different weights and with shorter shafts.

The mallet is a special wooden hammer. Heavier than the regular wooden hammer, it has a large flat area at both ends of the head. The mallet is very effective for working with wood chisels, because the shaft of the chisel will not be damaged by the wooden head of the hammer. The width of the mallet makes it less likely to miss the head of the chisel.

Experts in this field often use a special hammer to work on limestone. The limestone hammer has a small head with a flat edge on one end and a chisellike edge on the other. It has a long, springy shaft made from hazelnut wood. This hammer is used, for instance, to cut sections of limestone out of a bank. Usually, fossil collectors make a wooden frame corresponding to the size of the piece they intend to cut. They then gouge the stone around the edges of the frame and, with the chisellike edge of the hammer, strike the stone along the groove they have created. Collectors can usually tell by the sound of the hammer striking the stone when the plate has separated along the groove. At that point, the stone can be broken off easily. It is advisable to practice on a sample before attempting this on the real thing.

The plaster hatchet is a favorite tool of the fossil collector. One end is shaped like a hatchet; the other, like a hammer. This tool is particularly useful for separating layered shale sediments.

Some Useful Chisels

Chisels are used to break up, separate, or crush rocks. Those made from superior-quality steel that have a specially hardened cutting edge are most effective. Steel is hardened by exposing it to high heat, followed immediately by quenching it either in water or oil. The cutting edge of a chisel must be sharp. A dull edge usually separates the material in the wrong direction.

The head of the chisel, on the other hand, remains "soft." Over time, the edges of the head will curl under, "growing a beard" (56–3), which has to be removed from time to time to avoid injuries caused by metal splinters. With the constant pounding the head receives, the steel of the head begins to harden, and eventually the metal will splinter.

117

It is important that a chisel be positioned and held correctly. In addition, in order to protect the object that is worked on, the chisel must be struck appropriately. Keep your eyes on the cutting edge of the chisel, so that even the last blow won't have damaging effects. If you are worried that you will hit your finger, use a wooden mallet to soften the blow. Use heavy work gloves for protection, or protective sleeves, made specifically for chisels.

Attempting to remove deposits immediately surrounding a fossil with "one more try" often will result in either destroying the specimen altogether or breaking it into pieces. Fossil collectors call this extra try the "last blow." However, even with the greatest of care, fossils will break apart. Take heart in the fact that even the most experienced, professional collectors always keep a tube of rock glue close at hand.

In general, medium-size chisels, such as cross, flat, or pointed chisels, are sufficient for work done on location. Smaller, more delicate chisels are useful for the work done at home. Many collectors assemble their own set of chisels over time, sometimes making their own from steel nails or heavy needles. What is important are the cutting edges and the points. Cone-shaped chisels are less practical, since the stone might shatter in all directions.

The separating chisel, if correctly positioned and used with well-aimed blows, will separate material at the desired points. To separate large rocks, a separating chisel with a wide cutting edge is used. On location, this chisel is also used to shape a piece of rock for transport home. Using a variety of separating chisels and positioning the cutting edges on the predetermined line close together, the collector can separate a piece of rock precisely where he intends it to break.

The pointed chisel with a long tip is used to break rocks apart; however, it is not used in close proximity to a fossil because the danger of damaging it is great. The long, square-headed tip exerts more pressure forward than to the sides. The pointed chisel with a short tip exerts more pressure to the sides and is therefore well suited for work closer to fossils, particularly if there is only a thin layer to be removed. Applying water to this thin layer is very helpful. The flat chisel, with its straight, beveled cutting edge, is used for smoothing out rough surfaces. The blacksmith's chisel is similar in shape and is used for separating. The cutting edge of the cross chisel is beveled more on one side than on the other. The design helps to avoid any side pressure, which makes this the chisel of choice when attempting deep cuts.

For work that requires less intense pressure—for example, on fossils that are surrounded with hardened deposits—the wood chisel is ideal. The tool, intended originally for woodwork, is slanted on both sides and at the bottom edge. It has a somewhat flattened wooden handle that is secured on both ends by a metal ring, preventing the handle from splintering. A woodworker who uses this tool to carve wood only will shudder at the idea of using such a precious tool for rock shaping. The fossil collector, on the other hand, will very quickly consider it one of the essential tools and look for the best quality when buying one. The cutting edges need to be sharpened every time the metal is

Plate 56

1. Classic geology hammer. Full advantage of the design is taken when the hammer is held at the end of the handle.

2. Light mountaineer's hammer, used here to open a rock nodule.

3. Flat chisel with rolled-up edge at the head.

4. Crowbar with blunt edge works well on bowl-shaped surfaces, such as the inside of this oyster shell.

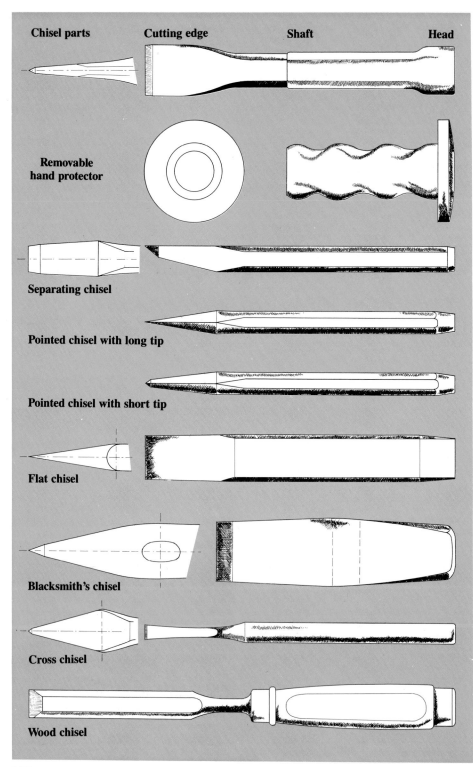

Chisel parts   Cutting edge   Shaft   Head

Removable
hand protector

Separating chisel

Pointed chisel with long tip

Pointed chisel with short tip

Flat chisel

Blacksmith's chisel

Cross chisel

Wood chisel

nicked, which is best done in a tool shop. In order to avoid striking this "chisel substitute" too hard, it is advisable to use a wooden mallet. Care is needed when working on bowl-shaped fossil surfaces, since the corner of the tool can easily cause damage (56–4).

The fossil collector can gain valuable support from other tools in the workshop: drills, sandpaper, discs, saws, etc. A vibrating motor tool (57–1) and a motor tool with a flexible shaft and variously shaped attachments (dental drills, etc) (57–2) are excellent additions to the toolbox of a fossil collector. While electric tools are time-savers, a professional will always reach for hand tools like the scraper and needle for the really delicate work. Everyone who collects and prepares fossils will find that chisels are the most effective tools.

Preparation with Knife and Needle

An all-purpose pocket knife like a Swiss army knife is an indispensable part of the fossil collector's toolbox. If used on location to pry away a rock, however, this knife can collapse, inflicting ugly injuries. Rigid or adjustable knives have proven to be much safer, particularly if they have a hand protector to keep the hand from slipping beyond the handle and onto the blade, as a hunting knife does. Time and again, severe injuries have occurred when a sharply pointed knife slipped while a collector was trying to remove deposits from a fossil the collector was holding in the palm of his hand (58–1). Here utmost care is essential. Fossils imbedded in

soft limestone plates (like oil shale from Messel) or still damp, soft layers of marl (like layers of plants from the Miocene period), where the earth is fresh and damp, require the use of a knife. When preparing the specimen, scraping and scratching can also be done with the knife blade. It is also useful for spreading and smoothing glue and putty.

A serious preparator of fossils takes particular pride in his or her preparation scraping knives, which are made from the finest flat steel, set into wooden handles. Holding the scraping knife in your right hand (if you are right-handed), scrape it in a leftward motion away from you so that the spot or area still to be scraped can be observed with ease (58–2). The preparation needle is equally as highly regarded. It is also made of the best available steel. The fossil collector is well served by a steel needle and phonograph needles that are inserted into or attached to wooden handles. However, when used with too much force, a needle may bend and damage the fossil. Sharply pointed needles and blades that are inserted into holders are also well suited for delicate work (58–3).

Sharpening, Grinding, Filing, and Rasping

In order for tools to be in good condition, they need constant attention. For rough filing, a hand-held grinding machine might be suitable. However, the cutting edge of chisels should not be allowed to heat up, since they would lose a great deal of their hardness. The best results are achieved when the edges are moved across a flat grinding stone. A grinding motor tool might also be used to remove the rolled-up edge on a chisel head; a metal file, however, is also effective. Rasps and files can be very helpful for smoothing out rough edges of a stone plate, to give the finished work a final touch.

Illus. 26: Useful chisels

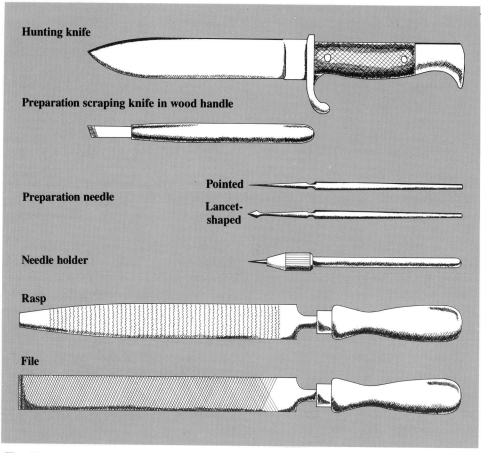

Illus. 27. Useful knives, needles and files.

Shaping

In my opinion, a fossil collector will always pay a high price for being careless when cutting a stone plate to size: damaged or destroyed fossils and additional work to put the pieces together again. We are better off if we follow the example of the people who shaped the limestone blocks in Solnhofen, or if we follow the methods used by the people who lay tiles: they scratch a groove into the stone with light taps of a chisel and break the plate either over the edge of a tabletop or with a few gentle taps along the precut groove.

Plate 57
1. Using a vibrating motor tool to prepare a fossil.
2. A drill with a flexible shaft and different attachments for brushes, drills, and chisels makes fossil preparation much easier.
3. Handpiece for dental drill with chisel tips, being used to extract an ammonite, *Taramelliceras*, 1½ inches wide (4 cm), embedded in limestone from the White Jurassic.

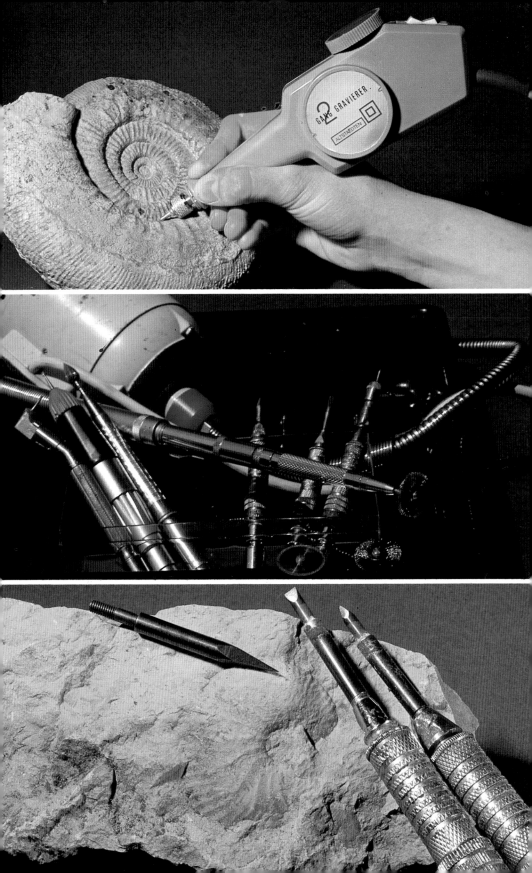

Another method is to use a pair of nippers and, piece by piece, break off material until the desired shape has been reached (58–4). The advantage of using tile-cutting pliers is that more pressure can be exerted, because of the tile-cutter's smaller mouth and relatively long handles. Breaking stone plates should be practiced first on plates that do not contain fossils.

Having learned from experience, a fossil collector will usually take home fossil-containing rocks that are much larger than the fossil itself. That holds true most of all for fossils embedded in rock plates like Poseidon Shale and limestone plates. At home, in a quiet hour the collector can examine the finds and mark off the excess with a metal point and a ruler. Depending on the hardness of the material, the excess can be removed with a hacksaw or special corundum saw (all-purpose saw). A hacksaw is preferred for more secure handling. This process can be very time-consuming and strenuous when dealing with large pieces. For smaller pieces, the collector may use either a hacksaw or a folding saw.

It is not unusual to find a shop where the fossil collector can have rock pieces cut to size for a small fee. The collector can also buy a stone saw, one of the ones offered to stone collectors. From there, of course, to the next step is not very far. And the next step is

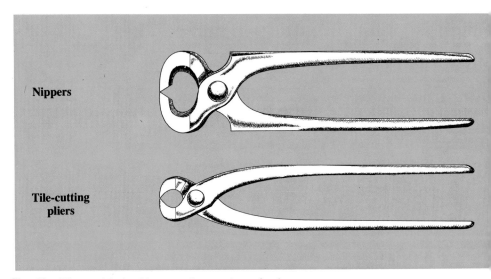

Nippers

Tile-cutting pliers

Illus. 28. Pliers used for breaking stone plates or pieces of rock.

Plate 58
1. Always move a sharp knife in the direction away from the hand and body.
2. The scraping knife is scraped away from you, so that the fossil can always be in sight. The fish *Leptolepis knorri*, 10 inches (25 cm) long, embedded in a limestone plate; Jurassic, Tithonian stage (Malm zeta), Solnhofen.
3. Tool-holder with inserts for piercing and scraping; ammonite *Amaltheus*, 1½ inches (4 cm) wide, after clay deposits were removed.
4. Excess from a thin stone layer is removed with a pair of nippers after grooves were made with a chisel or a saw blade. Here, a limestone plate with a belemnite from the Jurassic Pliensbachian stage is being shaped.

to buy the necessary equipment for grinding and polishing, which makes it possible to prepare beautiful specimens (59–1). Stone-trimming machines are available for shaping stone plates. A piece of rock is positioned between two opposite, chisellike steel bits, which move together slowly and steadily. This method permits well-controlled, slow and even pressure on the rock, which is im-

Cleaning Fossils

One of the saddest experiences occurs when a fossil is damaged or destroyed during the cleaning process. The fun of fossil collecting usually starts when, after vigorous brushing, a calcified or pyritized ammonite turns into an exemplary specimen. Delicate fossils and fossils without shells that are embedded in

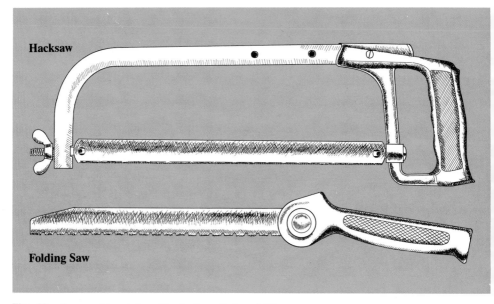

Illus. 29. Saws used to cut stone. *Top:* hacksaw. *Bottom:* folding saw.

portant because the rock almost always will separate in the direction of the applied pressure. When using a hand-held separating chisel, the rock usually splits in a direction that is not necessarily desired. The result of the latter method is that the fossil also breaks apart.

layers of marl are often destroyed when they are cleaned with a brush. This is particularly true for plant imprints. To find the best method, make a test on a similar piece of rock and try to find the safest way of cleaning. A vegetable-scrubbing brush is helpful in cleaning large, solid pieces. Cleaning larger,

Plate 59

1. Cross-section of a limestone-pyrite nodule, 3½ inches wide (9 cm), showing the ammonite *Pleuroceras'* shell and chambered phragmocone. The body chamber is filled with chalk.
2. Freed from deposits with the help of wire and brass brushes, a double-shelled oyster, *Lopha marshi* (Sowerby), with half a shell attached to it from a similar oyster.

hardened fossils with synthetic brushes and toothbrushes under water is effective for removing baked-on deposits. Wire brushes, particularly the soft brass and bronze brushes, when used with care, successfully

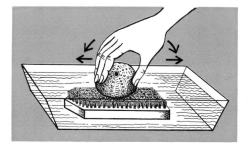

Illus. 31. Cleaning a fossil with a hard surface by brushing it across a bronze brush that is immersed in water.

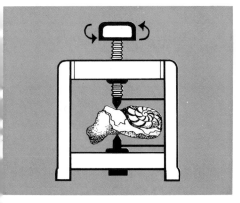

Illus. 30. Stone-crushing machine.

remove debris from hard fossil surfaces that don't have fine detailing (59–2). Limestone remnants are effectively removed when the fossil is moved across a bronze brush, 8×2 inches (20×5 cm) in size, with the bristles just barely covered by water (see Illus. 31). I use a soft brush (13–1) to remove loose, damp debris from delicate fossils. Blowing or brushing with a dust brush is sufficient for removing loose, dry dirt. Fossils hardened by silicic acid (SiO_2), like silica corals, can often be cleaned simply by being exposed for an extended amount of time to rain. In some cases a delicate but solid piece of fossil can be completely cleaned by immersing it in an ultrasound bath.

Large paleontology institutes usually have the most modern equipment. One of the most effective of these is the sandblasting apparatus invented by a Swiss professor, Dr. Kuhn-Schnyder. This apparatus is used to free delicate fossils, using either a fine-grained sand or crushed nut shells. Although it is time-saving and very gentle to the fossils, to prevent damage to the fossils, this method requires a high degree of concentration on the part of the collector.

Helpful Optical Tools

Good vision and, better yet, timely recognition of fossils at the location site are essential for a good fossil collector, because a fossil very seldom shows itself in full view. Often only small clues, like shell remains, round shapes, or a formation typical for a specimen indicate where a fossil might be hidden (31–1). A magnifying glass can be of great

Plate 60

1. *Platiceras niagarense*, a snail 1 inch (2.5 cm) long, with shell intact (Silurian period, Waldron, Indiana). It was prepared with a paper knife, needle, and wire brush. The snail was embedded in dense marl chalk.
2. *Pentremites godoni*, ½ inch (1.5 cm) long, embedded in marl, a blastoid from the Carboniferous-Mississippian period; found in Paint Creek shale, in Millistat, Illinois.

129

help. However, not until the collector is involved in the preparation of the fossil at home will he or she need optical tools. The position of the fossil and all the minute, important details have to be recognized early enough. Both a hand-held magnifying glass (62–1) and an illuminated magnifying glass are effective for examining relatively large fossils and give the observer a good overall view of the specimen. The object should not be magnified too much, however. A standing binocular magnifying glass (61), an illuminated magnifying glass with a flexible arm (Illus. 33), or binocular glasses worn on the head (optivisor) (62–1) are useful for working on large fossils.

When using such optical instruments, appropriate enlargement, for instance 1.5 × (6 diopter), is recommended. The lenses of the binocular magnifiers are easy to change if stronger magnification is necessary.

Collectors who prepare very small fossils will most likely not be able to work without a binocular microscope. This instrument gives the collector many different levels of magnification, or even continuous magnification of up to 40 ×, and makes the most minute details visible.

Many fossils are lost because they are not recognized. Attempts to detect fossils with the help of X rays have been made since the 19th century. But not until 1971, when a mobile X-ray unit was developed (by Prof. Wilhelm Stürmer of Erlangen) was it possible to examine large rock sections for fossils directly on location in the field. This method, of course, is not available for the average fossil collector. Furthermore, this method will only bring the desired results if the fossil shows organic changes that would serve as a contrast to the surrounding rock, such as the minute silicification that occurs in and around fossils contained in shale deposits. The electron microscope has given paleontologists a view of the most detailed, minute fossil remnants.

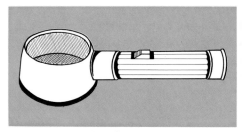

Illus. 32. Illuminated, hand-held magnifying glass, available in many different designs.

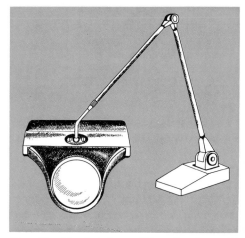

Illus. 33. Illuminated magnifying glass lamp with flexible arm. Many different models are available.

Photos taken on location of particular rock formations and fossils can be a great help, even many years later, in identifying fossils. My advice is to always take a camera with you on your fossil hunts.

A Workplace for Preparation

I cannot supply one specific recommendation for the fossil collector who wants to establish a work area. Lucky is the person

Plate 61
Preparation, using standing binocular magnifying glass.

130

who has a place set aside that is used for nothing but fossil preparation. Here he or she can work as often, as long, and as intensely as he or she wishes. When he or she leaves the work, everything will remain where it is and can be found where it was left. Personal preferences should not be interfered with; the work area will be for the collector what a studio is for the artist. I will share, as an example, the tools, instruments, and useful accessories that I gathered when I furnished my workplace in a small attic room.

For me, the table or work surface should be large, because in the course of preparation there is always something to be done and moved around—many rocks, tools, and accessories. On the table is a preparation box (Illus. 34), an old wooden box that has been soundproofed, similar to those used for electric typewriters. Since there are no aesthetic considerations here, a box constructed of old boards will do just fine. The back wall is high, and the sides are cut at an angle so as not to block out too much light. The top board is to catch rock splinters. The floor of the box can remain as is, but the sides and the top should be covered with foam or a similar material, because it will muffle the sound of splinters hitting the walls of the box. Any material that has soundproofing and cushioning properties will do, for example, rigid styrofoam blocks. A sheet of styrofoam, approximately ¾-inch thick (2 cm) is cut to cover the floor of the box. A sandbag is put on top of the foam sheet. The sandbag is made from a large piece of tough material and is filled with enough sand so that a rock or fossil can be nestled into it (as into a bowl)

with enough sand left to cushion the fossil underneath (62–2). I also like to use the cushioning material in which household appliances sometimes are packaged. Rocks stay securely in place and are well cushioned when placed on these hollow pieces of foam.

It is possible to strike a piece of rock forcefully without causing damage to the fossil. Hard pieces of rock can be wedged into a board cut out on one end for this purpose (62–4). The board is made from a thick piece of wood that has a wedge cut out at one end. The board needs to be secured to the tabletop with a clamp. A piece of rock can also be held, well-centered, in a vise, but not until the rock has been protected with cardboard on both sides. The rock will remain securely in place, something very advantageous when you perform detailed preparation work. Vises are easily available in hardware stores and come in many different sizes.

In close proximity to my work space is a piece of styrofoam, $2 \times 20 \times 40$ inches ($5 \times 50 \times 100$ cm), in which I can place tools like knives, needles, art brushes, and other small instruments in an upright position. Everything is at my fingertips, uncluttered; and everything can be quickly put away again (62–3).

Good vision is essential in order to perform good work. When it comes to preparing fossils, this is true for three different reasons: to protect one's eyesight, to be able to keep track of the work being performed, and in order to recognize early enough the position and condition of an embedded fossil.

For sorting and for performing rough work I use overhead 100 Lux fluorescent tubes.

Plate 62
1. Binocular magnifying glass (optivisor), worn on the head, and hand-held magnifying glasses.
2. On a sand-filled pillow, a piece of sandstone 6⅛ inches long (16 cm), containing a collection of belemnites from the Jurassic Toarcian stage (Liassic zeta) near Göppingen.
3. Tools and accessories in a styrofoam block for easy access.
4. A piece of rock containing a crustacean, *Pemphix sueuri* Desmarest, 3⅛ inches long (8 cm), from the upper shell limestone near Haigerloch, is wedged into a wooden cutout.

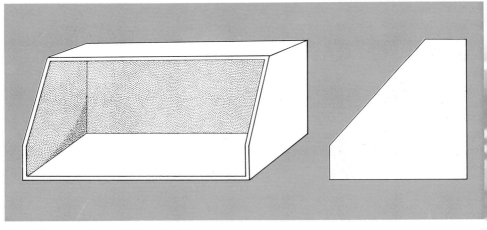

Illus. 34. Preparation box. *Right*: side view.

The recommendation for reading and writing, for instance, is 25 Lux overall illumination, and 500 Lux for direct illumination; and for monogram and goldsmith work it is 4000 Lux. For more detailed work, I have a gooseneck lamp with its own base that also can be screwed to the tabletop. Fiber optic bundles create perfect lighting when you are working with fine needles or removing deposits from very fine, detailed structures of very small fossils under a hand-held magnifying glass or an illuminated magnifying glass.

Above my worktable (which is about the size of a large desk) is a hanging motor tool with a flexible shaft, which is either suspended from the ceiling or attached to a wall-mounted bracket. Actually, it is a "retired" dental drill. If this drill has any feelings, it should be very happy to be in retirement, because its drill bits and brushes won't hurt ammonites or belemnites one little bit.

Used drills come in an endless variety of sizes and shapes. They all perform well as long as they are still sharp and are attached to a handpiece, which, in turn, is attached to the flexible shaft of the motor. The speed of the drill is regulated via a foot pedal. With the engine running quietly, and the hand piece

resting comfortably in my hand, often held like a pencil, I can fully concentrate on the preparation of the fossil in front of me.

This instrument is most often used at times when brass and wire brushes are needed. It also has small corundum sandpaper disks, ¾ inch (2 cm) in diameter, which are very useful for cutting small rock pieces, particularly if a fossil is in close proximity and could be damaged by a chisel (63–1). In addition, the handpiece can be equipped with a small, adjustable, pistonlike attachment. A small steel chisel can be inserted into this attachment (57–3). If the handpiece is used continuously, it is advisable to have a second one on hand, because a handpiece in continuous use tends to heat up.

Very few fossils are preserved in perfect condition. The collector who is looking for nothing but perfection will miss the "language" of the many fossils that are not. By "language," we mean the story a damaged fossil, or a fossil that has been distorted, is telling—the story of what transpired during its lifetime, or about life in primeval times in general, or about the changes that took place after the fossil had been imbedded. Such anomalies, like the effect of environmental influences on fish remains, or other unusual developments, can only be surmised from fossilized hard parts of an organism. Such pieces are a valuable addition to any collection.

It is a different story with fossils that were broken up due to a rock's fracturing, which can only be extracted in pieces. Dampness and humidity may have dissolved the rock surrounding the fossil, and perhaps the different fossil pieces cannot be glued together without leaving a seam. Nevertheless, putting them together again and reestablishing their former shape is an interesting project for every fossil collector. Many beautiful pieces displayed in museums have been glued and repaired.

A fossil collector can also piece together exemplary specimens for his or her collection (63–2, 63–4). That explains the presence of a mortar and pestle and a hand-held sieve on my worktable. I save rock splinters and samples from the deposits around a fossil in small plastic bags, to be ground up later when I want to repair a fossil or the material surrounding it. With the sieve, I separate the fine dust from the larger pieces, mix the dust with stone glue until it forms a thick paste, and use this paste to fill in ugly cracks and holes that otherwise would disfigure the specimen.

Adhesive tape is also very helpful. Often a beautiful specimen breaks apart as you are in the last stages of freeing it from the surrounding deposits. For instance, a lime-spar ammonite that I was determined, because of its rarity, to chisel out of the surrounding rock broke apart in not one, but six pieces. My positive attitude, so important for a successful undertaking, fell apart also. Should I glue the pieces together immediately? A professional would think twice! I usually put such pieces together with adhesive tape (63–3) and pack them carefully in a special carton, where the "seriously injured patient" will have to wait for the necessary operation. Sometime later, I schedule the day when I can undertake the rescue mission, reinvigorated and prepared to have fun with it.

In the extended sense, accessories are all those instruments, tools, and equipment that a fossil collector finds helpful and which make the work easier. Some of these I discuss in the sections on gluing and safety. It's useful to keep a roll of aluminum foil handy. When crumpled up, aluminum foil is an ideal surface for drying fossils that have been coated with a solution (64–1). Paper is usually not suitable for this purpose.

From Collecting to Displaying

Collecting and Preparing

The road from collecting a fossil to placing it on the display shelf can be short or long. Some pieces make it in a day; others take a year or decades. Sometimes, the trip can even take a century. There are immense amounts of fossils still in storage, part of a collection that is waiting to be examined, prepared, and identified. The reasons are the lack of personnel, the lack of space for display, and the lack of funds.

The fossil collector who has—more or less as a hobby, but nevertheless very seriously—searched for, collected, sorted, prepared, identified, and systematically organized and stored his or her fossils must someday thin out and examine the stockpile of rocks. In the beginning, every faint impression of a fossil will be the cause of great joy. But with increased experience (sooner or later, and in a few years at the most) he or she will be faced with an important decision. He or she must sort out the collection of rocks, a task which, according to an old tradition, must be undertaken at least 7 times on the road to a first-class, sensible collection. Another point: the collector must begin to specialize in a specific area of collection. The most sensible choice would be to concentrate on what locations nearby offer; but geological time periods or geographical locations can also be the basis for selecting a specialized field.

From the moment of collection to the time of displaying the fossil, the collector needs many different types of containers. On location, old newspaper is ideal for safely packing fossil-containing rocks. A knapsack or a sturdy bag with handles is often more suited for transporting heavier pieces. During the transport from the site to the vehicle, many a handle of a bag has broken, and sharp edges and corners have torn holes into many thin ones. Of course, every piece must be properly labeled with the locality and the type of rock formation where it was found. On location, one advisory should be followed: it is better to take home a large piece and examine and prepare it at leisure than it is to cut it too close and destroy a precious find.

Larger, thinner rock plates can be packed between two sheets of newspaper or foam, packed between two layers of cardboard, and then tied together (26–1). Clear plastic bags with airtight closures at the top are very practical for transporting and storing small, hard pyritized fossils. For extra safety during the trip home, these fossils can be wrapped in layers of newspaper. During the transport, as well as at home, the fossils should be protected against dampness and humidity.

Bags, plates, bowls, tumblers, cartons, and many other containers always pass through my workshop before they go into the trash. They make storage and sorting of the rocks and fossils much easier, and they are much appreciated during the preparation process. Once used, they can be easily discarded.

Small glass bottles and glass containers are very practical for preparing solutions and chemicals, such as paint and lacquer thinner, or acetone, which would dissolve most plastic containers.

At home, even if there is no time to examine the samples for usefulness, it is advisable to separate them according to the location where they were found. This avoids clutter. Old wooden vegetable or fruit boxes; empty sturdy cartons, no matter what their original use; and, of course, old containers from a laboratory or old trays are well suited for this, because stone, shale, and marl would make them unsightly anyhow.

In order to strengthen a carton, I put an additional layer of strong cardboard on the bottom. A sharp, serrated kitchen knife is handy and effective for cutting cardboard to size. Cardboard inserts are very good for other containers, too. In wooden crates cardboard covers possible cracks or spaces and the cardboard serves as a relatively soft cushion for the fossils.

Not until I have cleaned everything with a dust brush, brush, or water at home do decide which of the pieces I will prepare

Plate 63

1. Handpiece, to be attached to a flexible shaft motor tool, with a corundum sandpaper disk. Next to it is an ammonite, *Pleuroceras*, 1⅛ inches (3 cm) wide, with a coiled portion, partially cross sectioned.
2. Liassic ammonite, 18 inches wide (45 cm), with an almost totally destroyed surface. The broken pieces have been glued together.
3. A fractured belemnite held in place with adhesive tape.
4. The prepared underside of the same ammonite as above, *Arietites solarium* (Quenstedt), with few *Gryphaea arcuata* oysters attached to it, from the Jurassic Upper Sinemurian stage (Liassic alpha 3), from Aldingen, Swabian Alps.

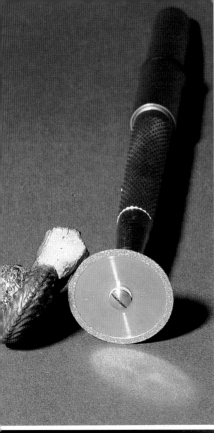

Without rushing, I cut the rock pieces with great deliberation and anticipation, and very often I will find small fossils that I did not know were there.

Waste is discarded in waste bins. Promising pieces, containing new types of fossils, or new specimens that seem in better condition than what I already have, are put in a bowl with a label recording the location where they were found. Everything else is carefully put in a folding box approximately 10 × 6 × 20 inches (25 × 15 × 50 cm). When empty and collapsed, these boxes take up very little storage space. I label the boxes, recording where the contents were found, the layer in which they were embedded, and the date they were found, and store them on shelves. Delicate pieces, for instance, plant remains embedded in soft marl or clay or pyritized fossils, should be protected beforehand to keep them from falling apart.

From Preparation to Display

Fossil collectors are lucky people. They train their intellects by delving into geological and paleontological subject matter. They keep their bodies fit by working in the field in fresh air. They have many successful experiences in discovering traces of the evolution of the planet. When looking at their prepared fossils, they experience joy at each individual piece that is protected from destruction.

To protect a fossil, the collector labels it immediately, even before he or she is finished working on it. The locality, rock layer, and date can easily be recorded on the back of the fossil with a waterproof pen (45–1) or on adhesive tape that is attached to the fossil. The information should also be recorded on an index file card (Illus. 36), which is assigned the same number that was recorded on the fossil itself. The number of the box in which the fossil is stored should also be included on the card. Fossils without identification are virtually worthless. To sum up,

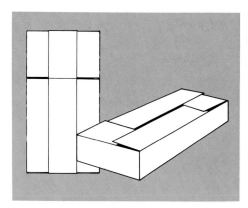

Illus. 35. Folding boxes can be assembled and closed when samples are placed in them.

for every fossil in a collection the following information should be available, if possible:

1. *Fossil identification:* genus and species and, if possible, the name of the author who first published information about its existence.
2. *Layer identification:* Period, epoch, stage, zone.
3. *Site of find:* Locality where the fossil was found: exact place, rock formation, ideally with land rights and elevation recorded from the respective topographical map (1:25,000), a sketch, and a note explaining if it was found in layered rocks or on an open slope.
4. *Year it was found.*
5. *Who found it, or from whom it was received.*

I prefer to keep a special card of the locality where a fossil was found. For amateurs (but also on occasion for professional paleontologists), it is extremely difficult to identify a fossil immediately after it is found. The reasons are international priority rights for fossils (where first publication counts), lack of appropriate literature, and often the lack of an overall view of the diversity of forms among the same group. It is helpful to find literature about specimens that were found in the same locality as your sample, visit the museum,

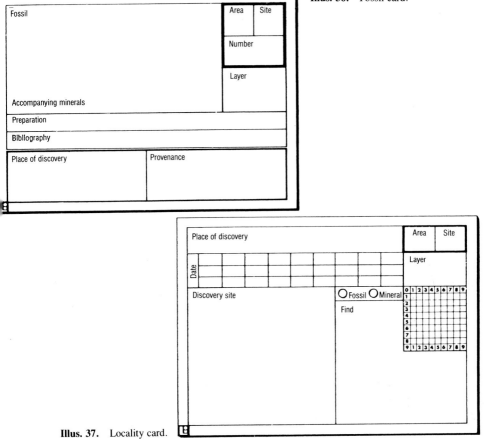

Illus. 36. Fossil card.

Illus. 37. Locality card.

make contact with experienced fossil collectors, and (last but not least) contact geological institutes and the scientists working in the field.

Not many excursions are necessary in order to accumulate fossils from different rock formations, perhaps even from layers dating from different periods in the earth's evolution, like the Jurassic, Cretaceous, or Tertiary periods.

Each location and each time period is represented by fossils that are worth preserving. For all the samples that have not yet been prepared, the fossil collector needs a suitable storage unit.

The ideal display and storage cabinet has not changed much in the last 100 years, ex-

cept for the material that is used to make it. For display purposes, you need a shelf arrangement on the top, either open or equipped with sliding glass doors, and as a base, a chest with drawers of a depth anywhere from 1.2 to 4 inches (3 to 10 cm).

A few very large fossils can be arranged decoratively on the floor or on an open shelf. Fossils make a greater impression when they are arranged systematically. Larger pieces belong in the back; smaller ones in front. Flat fossils can be displayed upright with small, clear, barely visible plastic cubes behind them so that they are presented in the proper light. Smaller fossils, such as small ammonites, can be held upright by pressing them against a small piece of nonhardening

139

plastic-based modeling clay (64–3). They can also be stored by suspending them in a wall cabinet; I have a specially made chest of drawers (64–5).

Someone who has been collecting fossils for decades might have a private fossil studio. This studio would not be used for rough preparation, but rather as an additional room for special research, for studying literature, taking care of professional correspondence, and for storing research notes and reports. This might also be the place where, in addition to housing the display cases, one could estab-

reports and the equipment for photographing fossils; and, of course, for a bookcase for literature. There should also be a place for an electron microscope to examine minute objects and delicate details of fossils.

All those specimens that are not going to be part of the exhibition also need a storage unit. Precious and sensitive fossils preserved on very thin rock plates—like those from the Jurassic period near Solnhofen, fish fossils from the Permian period, or trilobites from the Devonian period—have specially safe storage space in such a chest of drawers.

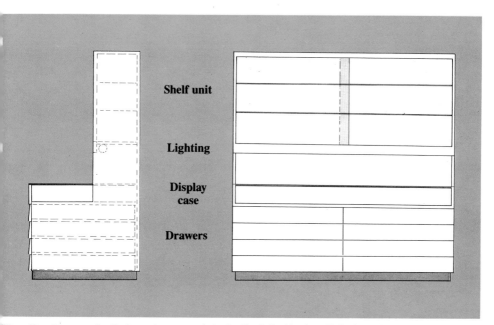

Illus. 38. Diagram of a display and storage unit for fossils. *Left:* side view. *Right:* front view.

lish a space for gathering fossils that are designated for a fossil exhibition; keeping

Separated by sheets of foam, fossils can be stacked on top of one another. Some precious

Plate 64

1. Aluminum foil is used as a surface for drying pyritized ammonites, which have been treated with a solution.
2. Fossil plate in an envelope lined with air-filled plastic bubbles.
3. Plastic-based modeling clay can be used to keep fossils in an upright position.
4. A bracket, fastened to the back with stone glue, allows this plate to be hung on the wall without a frame.
5. A wall unit with shallow drawers for storing small fossils.

1	2
3	4
5	

pieces are packed individually in cartons, others are wrapped in envelopes lined with air-filled plastic bubbles (64–2).

Fossil plates are often too large to store in chests of drawers. If the plates are strong enough, why not hang them, like pictures, on the wall? Mark the back of the plate near the top, where the bracket should be. To the

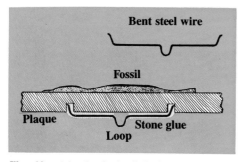

Illus. 39. A bracket for fossil display.

left and right of this point drill two ½-inch-deep (15-mm) holes, ¾ inch to 1⅜ inches (2 to 3 cm) apart, into the plate. Care must be taken that the holes do not go all the way through to the front. Shape a steel wire to form a bracket (see Illus. 39), with two extensions that will fit into the holes. Put the ends of the wire into the holes and attach them to the plate with stone glue. Be sure that both the left and right side arms of the bracket are also covered with glue. It usually takes no more than 10 minutes for the glue to cure

(64–4). To make sure that the plate is hanging parallel to the wall, glue small foam cushions to each corner of the plate. Plates prepared according to this method have been hanging on my wall for decades, for example, the plate with the fish fossil from Messel (19–2).

Hot-Cold Treatment as an Aid to Preparation

Nature makes sure that layers of earth and rock deteriorate over time, due to the influence of rain and periods of dryness, and cold and heat. This process, called weathering, generally destroys all fossils that are exposed. Fossil collectors can make the claim that it is they who are preventing the destruction of the fossils they find—and, if they do it properly, without disturbing nature and without killing plants or animals.

In the spring, after the last frost and after rain has washed away loose gravel, the fossil collector will find exposed fossils. Often these include ones that have been washed down from places that normally are not accessible. Nature has taken over the arduous work of extracting these fossils from the earth. Inevitably, a selection process has taken place: only hard fossils have survived.

Hard rocks become brittle through weathering, and solid, layered rock formations are easier to separate when they have gone through the winter season. In the spring, it is possible to split large pieces of rock that have

Plate 65

1 and 2. Fossils that are unsightly on the surface because of weathering often have a beautifully preserved underside. Here, *Homöoplanulites*, 12 inches (30 cm), from the Jurassic Callovian stage (Dogger zeta) from Albstadt, Swabian Alps.
3. Usually separated only by hot-cold treatment, hard, flat Tertiary rock layers from the Maar near Randeck.
4. Ammonite *Amatheus engelhardti* (D'Orbigny), 8¾ inches (22 cm), embedded in a layer of chalk near Göppingen, Swabian Alps.
5. Small fossils, securely embedded in plaster of Paris, are ready for preparation.

been lying around for centuries; often they split along the bedding plane.

It stands to reason to use this weathering process as part of the preparation process, particularly since this process is slower and gentler than the process of dissolving stone with chemical solutions.

A large ammonite, 12 inches (30 cm) in diameter, attached to a large piece of rock, had become unsightly due to influences during the embedding process. The ammonite was successfully removed after I left it exposed to wind and rain for one year. The back side turned out to be of flawless beauty (65–1, 65–2). Silicified fossils, particularly coral, can be freed from their surrounding deposits by rain, which dissolves the limestone. However, this process might take several years.

This weathering often makes the search for fossils on open rock, shale, or limestone slopes much more successful than hard work in similar, solid rock formations.

If plates cannot be split at home with a hammer and chisel, like the plates from the Maars, near Randeck (65–3), they can be exposed to extreme heat in the oven and then quickly immersed in cold water. The reverse is also possible: immersing frozen plates in hot water.

People who do fossil preparations professionally use different methods. For instance, they heat limestone in the flame of a Bunsen burner, which is supposed to loosen the fossil inside. However professionals also employ the hot-cold method, making use of the complete exchange of the air, present in every rock with water, and subsequently exposing the rocks to cold. They use this method when preparing large crystallized pieces of limestone.

The hot-cold therapy is most helpful when the fossil collector wants to split a fossil that contains another fossil. This process creates tension within the material. The task is accomplished by repeating the hot-cold treatment. The result can be hastened with a slight tap with a hammer. The "explosive" effect created by this process can be used to great advantage when dealing with small fossils, but larger fossils often fall apart when the rock surrounding them breaks apart.

Assembling Fossils

When visiting a museum of natural science we often look with amazement at the animal and plant fossils that have been prepared with attention to the most minute details. Usually we will see rock plates that have been reassembled to present an almost unblemished whole. At the museum, the fossil collector, properly impressed, is looking at the result of painstaking efforts that have taken months, sometimes even years.

Plate 66

1. An internal mold cast of a large (16-inch, or 40 cm) ammonite, *Lytoceras fimbriatum* (Sowerby). Several pieces were glued together to make it. Many inside coils were missing and have been reconstructed. The *steinkern* cast shows the living chamber and lobelines of the ammonite.
2. A glued-together limestone plate with a *Leptolepis sprattiformis*, 2⅜ inches (6 cm), and dendrites, consisting of manganese oxide. Glue particles, still visible, can easily be removed as long as they are fresh.
3. Fragile sandstone plate with traces of a brittle star, 1⅜ inches (3 cm). The plate was glued together on the back with a mixture consisting of stone, glue, and sand.

4. *Lytoceras* claystone *steinkern*, 8 inches long (20 cm), from the Jurassic Toarcian stage (Liassic zeta) from Mistelgau, near Bayreuth; it is held together with semigloss matte varnish.
5. Strengthened by preservation in glycerine, fruit of a *Tectocarya rhenana* Kirchheim, 1⅜ inches (3 cm) long, from the Miocene layers of brown coal decomposition near Zülpich.
6. Protective lacquer spray should be held sufficiently far away from the object when spraying, (12–16 inches or 30–40 cm), in order to avoid undesirable accumulation of the spray.

The fossil collector should recognize his or her limits and should not hesitate to seek advice from experienced collectors or (depending on the type of fossil discovered) to check with the geological institute in the area. For this reason, it is always advisable to join a local or national organization of people who share the same interests.

Experienced professionals will have the most useful suggestions, because their advice will be practical and effective.

When looking at fossils displayed in the museum, it is important to realize that most, if not all of these magnificent samples are pieced and glued together. Gluing broken fossils together requires courage on the part of the fossil collector, but that courage is acquired through experience, and once the collector feels comfortable, many a broken fossil can be taken home for repair. Very fragile fossils and those that have already broken apart may suffer additional damage on the way home. To avoid further damage, the collector must take some precautions.

We have no hard and fast rules for handling delicate or broken fossils during or after excavation or during the whole process of preparation, because the situations encountered and the conditions of each fossil and rock formation are so different. An embedded fossil is usually much better preserved on the underside, because that was protected from weathering. A good method to preserve this relatively undisturbed underside is to apply stone glue, plaster of Paris, or quick-drying glue to the weathered surface. Later, the collector can prepare the underside. The plaster of Paris or the glue can either be removed, or shaped into a base or a plate to display the fossil (65–4), depending on the condition of the fossil.

This method of dealing with fragile fossils at the location site can be expanded—for instance, for those fossils that the collector has securely embedded in a cast of plaster of Paris for safekeeping (65–5). First, the collector can work on one side; then he or she can reverse the process with a second plaster cast in order to work on the other side. Plaster of Paris mixed with carpenter's glue also works well for filling in cracks and missing portions of a structure.

Opinions are divided on the subject of whether or not those parts that have been replaced with a foreign substance should remain clearly visible. For me, there is no question. I come down on the side of aesthetics: I want the end result to be a fossil that is as pleasing to the eye as possible. This means that I use whatever is available and workable for repairing a broken specimen. Ultraviolet light will reveal where a fossil has been glued together.

Some clay marl layers from the Jurassic (Liassic gamma) contain large ammonites, *Lytoceras fimbriatum* (66–1), whose condition on the inside differs from that on the outside. The coil-shaped inner chambers are often missing or cannot be saved. The next structure, the *steinkern* with visible lobelines, has been preserved by pyritization; and on the outside, there is a *steinkern* cast with the compressed body chamber.

Carefully extracted and glued together, this ammonite, 16 inches (40 cm) in diameter, could be saved. The inner coil formation is a rough approximation.

Stone glue is available for many purposes, for industrial as well as home use. The one I use today might be replaced tomorrow by a better, more efficient product. The fossil collector needs a glue that will set in about 10 to 15 minutes, so that he or she can continue to work on the same piece without losing too much time. Since this glue consists of two components, the user can change the mixing ratio and modify the setting time and the hardness of the glue.

To avoid mistakes, I suggest that the fossil collector carefully read—and follow—the glue manufacturer's instructions. While one of the stone glues I am using will turn hard almost instantaneously after the stated 10 minutes, others (like a methyl methacrylate glue to which a hardening agent is added) dry more slowly, over time, and it is possible to work on an object during that drying period. Any residue left at the fracture joints (66–2) can be removed with a small knife or a needle without leaving any traces, before the glue has set up completely.

It is best to glue fragile, thin sandstone plates from the back, using a glue to which some sand has been added (66–3). In order to safeguard "fossil-nests" that are embedded in soft, claylike material, I let them dry out and then apply stone glue to the back and the sides. If the fractured pieces can be joined together without leaving a visible seam, clear adhesives won't leave any traces behind. Cracks, fracture seams, and the repair sites often are very unattractive and ruin the overall look of a fossil. However, these effects can be minimized if the collector adds dust, taken from a material similar to the one that is being repaired, to the glue. In general, stone glue is on the thin side and tends to run through the fracture site. Adding stone dust or a neutral filler to the glue thickens it and makes the job much easier. I sprinkle a little stone dust over the cracks and the places that have been filled in just before the glue dries completely, pressing the dust lightly into the surface.

Not every adhesive can be brought into contact with water. Glue might separate from stone that has become wet. However, some are water-soluble and will work on damp surfaces. I prefer to blend the glue into the surrounding area by, for instance, brushing it with a brass wire brush.

Many fossils break during the process of fossilization. This holds true most of all for belemnites, which are only found in one piece if they are very small (62–2). The only solution for those that are already broken is gluing (48). The process of gluing may take a considerable amount of time if the fossil is very large and has broken into 10 or more pieces (48–3), because one should only glue one fracture at a time. It is difficult to be exact when repairing a fracture under time pressure (32–3). Small pieces that might have splintered can be glued back at the location site, perhaps with rapid-drying glue. The advantage is that one does not have to search for the proper piece among many later.

The surface of a fossil can also be treated with a matte lacquer. This applies most of all for internal mold fossils that do not have shells and were embedded in softer layers. The 8-inch (20 cm) ammonite I found in a clay pit in Mistelgau near Bayreuth (66–4) was first allowed to dry before I saved it from destruction with a coat of lacquer.

Preservation and Preparation with Chemicals

For generations now, fossil collectors have been preserving fossils by soaking them in, or by covering them with, a layer of lacquer. Professionals advise against preserving delicate fossils with lacquer, because lacquer is not airtight. They point to numerous modern synthetic materials that are now widely available. Experimentation is the best teacher. Do have lacquer and acetone (for thinning) on hand. Shellac, because of its density, is the secret recipe of many a fossil collector. It has been used for generations, particularly for pyritized fossils. I have been using a mixture of 1 part shellac, 3 parts of lacquer, and 4 parts of acetone to protect my small, pyritized ammonites. As an extra precaution, I store them in plastic boxes to protect them from humidity.

Many fossils do not need any special conservation. Those that do need extra protection are exceptions, for example, porous bones or brittle mammoth teeth, which over time have lost their calcium content. Slow drying, avoiding exposure to direct sunlight, and additional conservation steps can make these objects durable again, preventing further deterioration.

A traditional conservation product is carpenter's glue (wood glue), which is combined with water and brushed on the fossil surface until the fossil is well impregnated. Drying time can be shortened between coats if the fossil is warmed. The glue, initially milky in appearance, will dry to a clear coating and makes the fossil impervious to humidity.

Bones that already have begun to fall apart and damp fruit remnants from the Tertiary period used to be immersed for a considerable amount of time in a glycerine bath (66–5, 68–1).

Modern plastics are available that dry very rapidly, so the work on a particular object will not have to be interrupted. Others take several hours to dry and are well suited for use on objects that have to be reassembled from pieces. Some plastics are equally effective for making an airtight coat on fragile fossils, preventing further disintegration, and for making casts (duplicating fossils). Duplicates of rare fossils, or those that are representative of a particular type, can be made available for teaching purposes, as additions to collections, or as treasures for hobbyists. They are almost perfect substitutes for real fossils.

Fossil cavities can now be filled with silicon rubber, soft casting dough, plastic filler, or plastic modeling clay to which a hardener has been added. This type of cast separates easily from dense rock surfaces and remains springy. In the past we used to use plastic modeling clay, plaster of Paris, or gutta percha; the latter remained springy when warm.

Plastics also make it possible to prepare fossils from the Eocene period, which were found in a condition which previously would have precluded any form of preservation. The methods are constantly being improved, with great success. In the section on fossils in oil shale (p. 37) I went into more detail about my own experience with this process. It is a process that can also be used for the preservation of difficult fossils, which we were unable to handle successfully, until now. Fossils from the limestone plates from Solnhofen can also be stabilized with plastic. The layer of lime then can be dissolved with a 5% solution of acetic acid. What remains is the fossil embedded in the resin. Treated in such a way, the fossil can be viewed from both sides.

There is no recipe for stabilizing delicate, or easily erased, often paper-thin fossil remains, or fossilized surface structures. Nevertheless, every experienced fossil collector and every professional in the field has his or her magic cure. What works for pastel drawings may also work for equally sensitive fossils: fixative. Easily available in spray cans, it not only preserves pastel drawings, but also the delicate remnants of a fossil.

Plant remnants from the famous Miocene layers near Öhningen (13, 39–3) and paper-thin plant remains [for example of coal or stone dust from the Rötolias or the Bayreuth and Kulmbach region (67, 39–1), as well as fossils from the limestone plates of Solnhofen (24, 26, 27)] can all be easily stabilized with matte lacquer.

It seems obvious, but nevertheless seems worth repeating: spray cans should not be

Plate 67
Delicate, colorful remains of *Podozamites lanceolatum* Göppert are embedded in layers of lenticular sand-clay, near Kulmbach. They were preserved with a layer of matte lacquer. Jurassic Rätolias, partial section, approximately 5½ × 4 inches (14 × 10 cm).

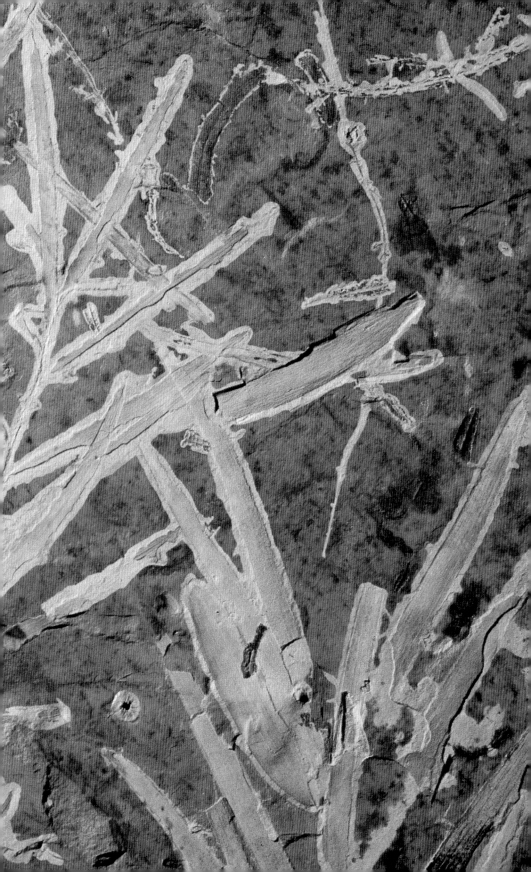

exposed to sunlight or put on a heating unit, because of the danger of explosion. In addition, lacquer spray and fixatives may be toxic, so be sure to use them outdoors or in a well-ventilated room. As has already been mentioned, the lacquer spray should be applied while holding the can about 12–16 inches (30 to 40 cm) away from the object to be sprayed. Too close means too much lacquer: too bad for the fossil! (66–6).

Experiment with new products on old pieces of fossil from the garbage bin. It won't be long until you too will have your very own secret recipe—and it is hoped that you too will share it with other collectors, perhaps as a thank you for help received in the past.

Large fossils that were surrounded by limestone often show signs of all the work that went into them; they are obviously lighter in some places, which may diminish the enjoyment of a piece (68–2). But fear not, there are fluosilicate waterproofing, flagstone-protecting products, which will be the answer. They change the surface of a fossil, leaving behind a dull or shiny wax coating. Difference in color and shade are lessened and the fossil looks good again (68–4).

Professionals advise against the use of fluosilicate on very small fossils—those smaller than 2 inches (5 cm)—and for those that have very delicate surface structures, particularly on those that have only microscopically visible markings. Fluosilicate erases those markings and structures.

Applying several layers of a hard wax, or car wax, is also very good. I do not use fluosilicate on pyritized surfaces because I feel that it encourages the process of "blooming" (15–4), the disintegration of pyrite (FeS_2) into sulfuric acid, iron oxide, and white, powdery iron sulfate (see pages 33 and 34).

Before the fossil collector begins the actual work with chemical substances, he or she should first consult the relevant literature and/or seek the advice of experienced colleagues. After all, handling acids and bases is not without its dangers. I highly recommend wearing protective gloves, protective glasses, or goggles and working in a place with good ventilation. A first-aid kit with eyewash, and something to absorb spills (like kitty litter) should be nearby.

Among all the available methods is one the fossil collector uses most often: extracting silicified fossils from limestone with diluted acetic acid. Acetic acid will be less likely to injure you or your fossils than stronger acids. Any work with acid should be supervised closely as it progresses, so you don't destroy your fossil.

The choice of which chemical compound to use to dissolve the stone surrounding a fossil is based on the chemical composition of the fossil and its surrounding material. Consult specialized literature and contact experts in museums for information as to which to use. It is necessary to protect the exposed

---

Plate 68

1. A pine cone, *Pinus brevis* Ludwig, 2 inches (5 cm) long, from the Miocene period, from the brown-coal mining region Victor, near Zülpich.

3. Tower-shaped turrilites (a kind of ammonite) are peculiar to the Cretaceous period. Here, a large find of a *Turrilitoides saxonicus* from the chalk limestone of Turon from Gross-Elbe near Baddeckenstedt.

2 and 4. Ammonite *Sonninia sowerbyiadicroides* Hiltermann 6¾ inches (17 cm) wide with chisel marks. After an application of stone dust and fluosilicate waterproofing chemicals (bottom), this specimen is an acceptable piece for the display case. From the Jurassic Bajocian stage (Dogger gamma), Swabian Alps.

fossil as you work, and to recoat it with an acid-proof chemical as more fossil is exposed.

Preparation of Microfossils

Chemical compounds are not only used to free large fossils; they are also used to free very small fossils whose study requires the use of a microscope, called microfossils. Chemicals dissolve stone, and in the "stone mush" many microfossils can be found.

Those who have searched for gold are familiar with the method used to separate heavier from lighter materials. The collector of microfossils uses a similar method. In a container, he or she mixes stone mush with water. Lighter particles will float to the top; heavier materials sink to the bottom.

The stone mush is put through sieves with successively smaller holes. In the end it is put through a fine cloth. At the end of this process, microfossils are left in the cloth. With the help of a magnifying glass (× 50 enlargement is sufficient) or a stereomicroscope, the collector will get a close view of the world of microfauna, including cyanobacteria, calcareous algae, diatoms, and radiolarians.

Microfossils can be cut into transparent disks .2–.3 mm thick; in this way they can be examined, recognized, and identified, making it possible to gain a much more profound insight into the composition and structure of microfossils, as well as of all fossils.

The microscopic research conducted into the world of primeval times (in combination with new, special equipment and the constant improvement in techniques) has brought, and still is bringing, new knowledge and new methods of preparation.

Dangers and Means of Protection

Anybody who handles stones must protect himself from them. To find this sentence in a book that talks about preparation might be surprising. However, I must emphasize the dangers to which a fossil collector is exposing himself or herself, since preparation begins when fossils are extracted. I am writing this in memory of my friend Günter Löchl, as he would have wished. As a fossil collector he gave an impeccable example, but nevertheless he lost his life in a rock slide while searching for fossils with a friend from France. Never underestimate the danger that outcroppings represent, regardless of whether you are on top or below them. Often we dig deep holes or hollow out soft slopes. These holes leave ugly scars on the landscape, and they entice the next person to continue to dig where the person ahead of him may have escaped danger only through sheer luck. Owners of such areas may prohibit further activities. Fossil-rich areas, known for a century, have been lost to collectors.

Even small stones and rocks can cause considerable injuries when you search for fossils on slopes. Safety helmets are an absolute must for collectors. They should be part of the basic equipment of every fossil collector. Furthermore, great caution is called for when working above or below another collector, because tumbling rocks have caused many an ugly injury.

The hands of the collector also need pro-

Plate 69
1. Strong gloves provide protection against injuries from stones; rubber gloves protect against dangerous solutions and glue.
2. Tools marked with colored tape are easy to find.

tection (69–1). Rough, strong gloves should be used when working with a hammer and chisel, to help in avoiding injuries from stone splinters and from sharp edges. When working with acids, rubber gloves are a must. I also recommend having a first-aid kit close at hand at all times, including eyewash, and making sure that your tetanus vaccination is up to date.

When cutting or chipping stone, it is imperative that eye protection be worn. One look at my scarred safety glasses proves how important this is. Of course, safety glasses or goggles should also be worn when other things might endanger your eyes; for instance, when you are working with acid solutions. When it comes to toxic fumes, I have only one recommendation: fresh air! Ideally, one ought to work with them only outdoors. Store and use chemicals and tools where children can't get at them. Dust respirators should be worn to filter out dust generated in preparing a fossil.

Aside from protecting oneself, one's companions, and the fossils that have been collected, it's good to protect one's tools. I am not referring to the safe and efficient way that hammers, chisels, or knives ought to be handled. Rather, I am thinking of protection against losing tools, and the avoidance of long searches at the digging site, particularly when the tools are covered with wet clay or marl, or when a tool has fallen over an outcropping, which makes detection difficult. I have lost many tools and found many that belonged to others. Since I decided to mark all my tools by painting the handles a bright red, or by covering them with bright red tape or reflecting tape (69–2), detection has been much easier. Hopefully, I won't lose them anymore. I always try to put my tools down in the same place, such as on a piece of newspaper or a tool bag, but in a moment of excitement, those good intentions are usually forgotten.

The tools mentioned in this book are available in almost any specialty store. Information about such shops is usually listed in the classified section of professional magazines and journals.

Bibliography

Anderson, J. G. C. *Field Geology in the British Isles: A Guide to Regional Excursions.* Elmsford, New York: Pergamon Press, 1983.

Black, Rhona. *The Elements of Palaeontology*, 2nd ed. Cambridge University Press: Cambridge, New York, Melbourne, Sydney, 1988.

Burns, Jasper. *Fossil Collecting in the Mid-Atlantic States.* Baltimore, Maryland: Johns Hopkins University Press, 1991.

Castell, Cox. *British Caenozoic Fossils.* Trustees of the British Museum of Natural History: London, 1975.

Converse, Howard H., Jr. *Handbook of Palaeo-Preparation Techniques*, 2nd ed. Florida Paleontological Society: Gainesville, Florida, 1989.

Morrison, Reg, and Morrison, Maggie. *Australia: The Four-Billion Year Journey of a Continent.* New York: Facts on File, Inc., 1990.

Rayner, Dorothy H. *Stratigraphy of the British Isles.* New York: Cambridge University Press, 1981.

Rich, P. V., and Van Tets, G. F. *Extinct Vertebrates of Australia.* Princeton, New Jersey, Princeton University Press, 1991.

Thompson, Ida. *The Audubon Society Field Guide to North American Fossils.* New York: Alfred A. Knopf, 1982.

Plate 70
At a site in Altmühl Valley, searching for fossils in fossil-bearing limestone layers.

Index